Disentangling

from

Emotionally
Immature People

Avoid Emotional Traps, Stand Up for Your Self, *and*
Transform Your Relationships *as an* Adult Child
of Emotionally Immature Parents

LINDSAY C. GIBSON, PsyD

New Harbinger Publications, Inc.

Publisher's Note

All stories in this book have permission to be used and are heavily disguised to preserve anonymity. In many cases, details have been combined to create composite accounts. Names and identifiable details have all been changed, so any resemblance to real people is purely coincidental.

This work in no way should be construed as a form of psychotherapy. Its purpose is educational only and it's designed for the entertainment purposes of increasing self-knowledge and the understanding of people. The ideas in this work are based on psychological insights and clinical observation and represent the theories of the author from a career as a psychotherapist. Readers are responsible for seeking professional therapeutic help as needed, and the author and publisher make no representation of this work as a substitute for psychotherapy or clinical consultation.

NEW HARBINGER PUBLICATIONS is a registered trademark of New Harbinger Publications, Inc.

New Harbinger Publications is an employee-owned company.

Copyright © 2023 by Lindsay C. Gibson
New Harbinger Publications, Inc.
5720 Shattuck Avenue
Oakland, CA 94609
www.newharbinger.com

Cover design by Sara Christian; Interior design by Michele Waters-Kermes; Acquired by Tesilya Hanauer; Edited by James Lainsbury

---

Library of Congress Cataloging-in-Publication Data

Names: Gibson, Lindsay C., author.
Title: Disentangling from emotionally immature people : avoid emotional traps, stand up for your self, and transform your relationships as an adult child of emotionally immature parents / Lindsay C. Gibson, PsyD.
Description: Oakland, CA : New Harbinger Publications, [2023] | Includes bibliographical references and index.
Identifiers: LCCN 2023002852 | ISBN 9781648481512 (trade paperback)
Subjects: LCSH: Self-confidence in adolescence. | Self-help techniques for teenagers. | Adult children of dysfunctional families--Mental health. | Emotional maturity. | Dysfunctional families--Psychological aspects. | BISAC: SELF-HELP / Personal Growth / General | PSYCHOLOGY / Interpersonal Relations
Classification: LCC BF575.S39 G524 2023 | DDC 158.1--dc23/eng/20230317
LC record available at https://lccn.loc.gov/2023002852

Printed in the United States of America

26   25   24

10   9   8   7   6   5   4   3

To Skip, with all my heart.

To my clients and readers over the years,
who have made this work possible.

Contents

Part III: Stepping Back

Part IV: Saving Yourself

Part V: Solving Problems

Appendices

Introduction

You have something inside you that knows what is right and healthy for you—and what isn't—even if you lack the words or concepts to explain why. This internal sensing system tells you, through emotional and physical warning signals, when something is wrong or you're being mistreated. Since childhood, this wordless center in you has recorded the truth of your experiences in its language of memories, emotions, and symptoms. Now's your chance to decipher it.

It's been amazing to me how instantly my readers have resonated with the phenomena of what it's like to be an adult child of emotionally immature parents (ACEIP) and to have to deal with emotionally immature people (EIPs) in general. It was as if they had had a piecemeal awareness of what was going on but hadn't yet conceptualized what they knew. They were missing the theoretical framework that could help them consolidate and finally understand the relational experiences they had lived through.

In this book, we're going to give your implicit knowledge a voice. As you read, you will find out what your feelings were trying to tell you, as pieces of your experience click into meaningful place. These feelings will no longer silently burden you; they will become conscious, understandable experiences you can grow from. You will have gained objectivity and room to think.

You also will be able to reconsider self-protective childhood behaviors you may have learned to avoid conflict, and reassess how you want to handle emotionally immature (EI) pressures from now on. You may have adapted to EIPs in your early life, but once you become aware of their predictable dynamics, you can change your approach and emotionally protect yourself. You are not duty bound to remain entangled with them. You don't have to keep following their directions, nor do you have to feel guilty for changing course. You can decide what's best for you.

This is the fourth book in a series that began with *Adult Children of Emotionally Immature Parents*. The structure of this book is based on the kinds of questions that repeatedly come up in my therapy and life-coaching sessions with clients who are dealing with EIPs in general, and especially with entanglements with EI parents. (Throughout the book, I will use "EIP/

EIPs" for any emotionally immature person or people, and will specify references to EI parents separately.) Please use this book as a kind of handbook in which you look up answers to issues that concern you the most.

Feel free to jump in wherever you want. Scan the table of contents or index to see what catches your eye to work on. With this book you will learn to build self-confidence, set boundaries, and establish a more empowered relationship with EIPs in your life.

My hope for you is that this book will spark realizations that will explain you to yourself. I am going to try to put into words what you may already know—what you've sensed but haven't articulated—while giving you ideas for how to improve your approach to life and relationships, not just with EIPs but with everyone. Hopefully you will gain transformative self-knowledge and insight, which are essential catalysts for positive change. Our goal together is to help you disentangle yourself from other people's unfair expectations and emotional traps. Our work will support your individual identity and reconnect you with that lively, interesting self of yours.

Along the way, I'll contrast emotional immaturity with emotional maturity, so you'll see what each is like. When I mention emotional maturity, keep in mind that a person can have more or less of it. That's why I refer to people as being "adequately" or "sufficiently" emotionally mature. Maturity is not an endpoint achievement, but a work in progress—a lifelong creation.

This book is divided into five parts. In parts I and II, you'll learn about emotional immaturity and maturity, what motivates EIPs, and how EIPs impact your life. Part III will show you the importance of stepping back to reposition your relationships with EIPs and to reevaluate how much energy you want to give them. In part IV, you will learn how to change those self-defeating beliefs you internalized from people who told you what to do and how to be. Finally, in part V, we'll explore solutions to the thorniest dilemmas that come up both internally and in your relationships with EIPs.

In addition to strategies for dealing with EIPs and their impact on your life, you'll find "Reflection and Discovery" sections in each chapter. These contemplative exercises will move you deeper into self-discovery and help you become more self-confident, self-attuned, and clear about your goals as you chart a new course in life. Due to the size limitations of this book, there may not be enough room for you to write as freely and fully as you'd like, so consider using a separate journal for more space as needed. Each chapter ends with a helpful tip, a little reminder to nudge you in the right direction.

As mentioned in the publishing credits, this book is not psychotherapy and is surely not a substitute for therapy. Please monitor your reactions to what you're reading so that you can avoid feeling overwhelmed or triggered. Be sure to seek therapy and support as needed. The optimal use of this book would be for you and your therapist to use it as a supplement to your therapy.

If you so choose, EIPs can be a *part* of your life, but they shouldn't be the main *focus* of your life. They may insist on being center stage—their immaturity demands it—but you don't have to agree to be their willing audience. EIPs can set you on a life course of attending to other people's demands at the cost of your emotional health. You can decide anytime that this pattern is not for you and change direction instead. Contrary to their objections, being true to yourself is *not* the same thing as being unfair to them.

Whether you identify as an ACEIP yourself or are a therapist interested in helping ACEIPS—or both—you can use this book to understand what ACEIPs go through and how it shapes their responses to life. You will learn both practical tips and deeper strategies that will help support your or your client's emotional needs and personal individuation.

I hope you come away from this book with a deeper appreciation of your emotional gifts and sacred individuality, while seeing your strengths with new accuracy. I hope you realize that it's not just your basic *needs* that are important, but your *preferences* as well. Your preferences form the basis of your unique individuality and deserve your respect and protection. Instead of devoting your energies to pleasing and placating EIPs, you can change course to be more in alignment with who you are.

Are you ready for your course correction? I'm ready to bring you all I know.

Part I

Why EIPs Are
the Way They Are

How would I know if someone was emotionally immature?

Hallmark traits of emotional immaturity

Emotional immaturity encompasses a wide range of personality styles. People can be very different yet still show the traits of emotional immaturity. This syndrome is not a type of mental illness, and ordinary, "normal" people may show its signs. People with psychiatric diagnoses often have underlying immaturity, but not all EIPs qualify for a psychiatric diagnosis. A person's EI traits become especially noticeable when stress increases or relationships become more intimate.

Emotional immaturity is easier to recognize if you focus on the basics (see appendix A for a summary of EI features). Although emotional immaturity exists on a continuum of severity, the following five characteristics are foundational in all EIPs, independent of their personality type or level of functioning:

Egocentrism is the basis of the EIP's orientation toward life. Like young children, they primarily view the world through their own self-preoccupations and swiftly entangle you in their expectations.

With such a self-centered approach, EIPs have *limited empathy* for others. They don't put themselves in other people's shoes nor imagine their inner experience. While they may be intelligent and socially skilled, they don't feel for other people so much as sense advantage and opposition. This is why an EIP can be an admired or powerful figure in society, yet still have trouble relating to other people in an adequately mature way.

Although EIPs may be plenty smart, they avoid *self-reflection*. Self-justifying and often self-righteous, they rarely question themselves. They focus on their immediate emotions and desires, seemingly oblivious to how they're impacting others or even their own future. Instead of reflecting on their behavior, they get defensive and double down on their own position if someone gets upset with them.

When it comes to getting close to other people, EIPs pull back from *emotional intimacy*. They have a hard time accepting heartfelt emotion from others and certainly have trouble giving it. They may seem highly emotional when they blow up or lose emotional control, but that's not the same as emotional intimacy. Emotional intimacy occurs between two people who share and process emotional information with each other, getting to know one another at a deep level. This process need not even be in words; it can be the sense one feels that the other person "gets" you and can connect with you in a deeply authentic way. In contrast, EIPs are more likely to become defensive, evasive, or belligerent when others (including their children) try to relate to them with emotional openness and honesty. (You can imagine the negative effect this kind of response has on a young child seeking connection.)

In their approach to the world, EIPs use *affective realism*, defining reality as what they *feel* it to be (Barrett and Bar 2009). Their psychological coping mechanisms are immature (G. Vaillant 2000) and simplistic, especially as they deny, dismiss, or distort any reality they don't like. Their lack of rational objectivity means that it's nearly impossible to reason with them once their emotions take hold.

Now let's look at some additional characteristics. Some EIPs are extroverted and dominant, while others are more introverted, passive, and dependent. But whatever their style, EIPs tend to be rigid, superficial, rather shallow personalities. They often express themselves in platitudes or clichéd sound bites that are lacking in real thought. They are not well integrated psychologically, meaning that conflicting aspects of their personality coexist with no awareness of contradiction. They can say one thing and do another with no embarrassment because they don't notice the mismatch. They focus on the immediate "part" of a situation, not its whole meaning.

Emotionally, they live in the present moment, blurting the first thing that comes to mind and reacting with no regard for the long-term effects of their impulsivity. Their high reactivity also means they are easily overwhelmed, making any problem feel like an emergency to them.

EIPs think in simplistic, literal, black-and-white terms. Logic tends to be used mostly as an opportunistic weapon, not as an essential determinant of their thinking. They typically oversimplify complex topics in ways that make it hard to reason with them.

Actively dominant EIPs overrun other people's ideas and boundaries. Many are very status and role conscious, expecting others to keep to their assigned roles. Even a more passive and acquiescent EIP won't show much empathy or interest in your life. Your subjective experience just doesn't register with them. They expect you to mirror their moods: if they're happy or upset, you should be too.

EIPs jump to conclusions and easily take offense, making it extremely hard—if not impossible—to talk out problems and disagreements. In conversation, they don't listen well because, like children, they are always vying for center stage. When communicating, they are set on "broadcast" rather than "receive." They have little curiosity for your viewpoint and feel affronted and unloved if you don't do what they want.

More dominant EIPs have low stress tolerance, tend to be impatient, and pressure others to give them what they want. They expect their relationships to revolve around their reactive emotions, and they relate primarily through pronouncements, controls, and demands. Impatience plus egocentrism means that they take things personally and blame everything on other people. EIPs also can be irrationally stubborn, with hair-trigger defensiveness toward anything that threatens their beliefs or self-esteem. They are prone to meltdowns, making people around them feel rushed, criticized, and fearful of upsetting them further. The more passive EIPs may not be as flamboyant emotionally, but underneath their relatively calm demeanor lurks an implacable egocentrism concerning their agendas and motivations.

In close relationships, EIPs expect others to stabilize them emotionally and prop up their self-esteem. The burden of maintaining peace in the relationship usually falls to the other person because EIPs don't do the emotional work (Fraad 2008) necessary to keep relationships on an even keel. Insensitive to others' feelings, they think that love means giving blanket approval and letting them do whatever they want. Like a young child, an EIP gains power by distressing others until they capitulate. After funneling your attention into an EIP, you'll probably come away feeling depleted and drained of energy.

Even the quieter EIPs are instinctively emotionally coercive, controlling you with guilt, fear, shame, or self-doubt. Unless you give in, they will peg you as bad or untrustworthy, and if you do something they don't like, they will confide in other people against you rather than dealing with you directly.

Whether EIPs demand your attention and self-sacrifice or quietly expect you to prop them up, they have a hard time accepting love. When you act lovingly toward them, they act as if they can't stand to let it in. With such poor *receptive capacity* (L. M. Vaillant 1997), they are like a distressed child who won't let their parent soothe them. The closer you try to get to them, the more they pull back. This is because emotional intimacy threatens to overwhelm and disorganize them. Their fear of emotional intimacy often comes out in irritability, provocations, or conflicts that forestall closeness or vulnerability.

Because EIPs project blame onto other people, you might unwittingly accept their confusing distortions and take responsibility for things that weren't your fault. Therefore, it is critically important to maintain healthy detachment and think objectively about their behavior.

Let's look at some strategies and reflections that can help you identify the EIPs in your life.

Strategy

Did you recognize any of those EI characteristics in the difficult people in your own life? If you like, you can go back and circle the characteristics that fit. Some EI features are less apparent in more introverted or passive EIPs, so in trying to determine if someone fits the EI mold, you might try focusing more on their underlying motivations and view of the world than on overt behaviors.

Your next step is to consider if someone's emotional immaturity has affected your self-image and life choices. Emotional immaturity has an interactional impact, becoming most obvious in relationships where your self-worth is at stake. As we'll see later, the way EIPs protect themselves comes at a cost to others.

Reflection and Discovery

Think of a person who you think might be emotionally immature. How do you feel about considering this person emotionally immature? For instance, do you feel disloyal or unfair, or find it to be a relief? Write down your feelings about this so you have a baseline for later.

_____

_____

How have this person's EI traits affected your confidence and sense of lovability? Which EI characteristics have been the hardest for you to deal with?

_____

_____

Tip: Because EIPs seem so sure of themselves, their rigid attitudes can suggest strength, passion, or moral righteousness. Their insistence on being right can intimidate you into allowing them to dominate you. In many interactions, you may reflexively doubt yourself when they get threatened and defensive. Understanding these dynamics allows you to not fall under their spell. Your knowledge of them is your power. Awareness of emotional immaturity keeps you informed and self-possessed when you have to deal with any difficult person who tries to take you over.

2

How can my grown-up parents be immature?

Understanding emotional immaturity

Tanya had a hard time thinking of her parents as emotionally immature. When I gently suggested it, she looked like she thought a lightning bolt might cleave my office at any moment. She stared at me in disbelief: "How could they be immature? They ran their own business; they sent us all to college. I know they love me, and they took good care of us when we were sick. They are the most moral people I know!"

I brought up emotional immaturity only when I could see that Tanya wasn't going to find answers to the problems she was seeing me for without considering this alternate understanding of her parents. Tanya was dubious, but she warily followed my reasoning on why I thought her parents seemed emotionally immature. It would be many weeks before Tanya was willing to explore her parents' immaturity and the suffering it had caused her. I didn't pressure her because I know how preposterous it can seem to think of your parents as less mature than yourself. Tanya and I first needed to agree on what the problem was before we tried to solve it together.

In contrast to Tanya, some clients are relieved to have a name for their parent's behavior. Everyone's different. But if parental immaturity is part of the picture for someone, I believe it has to be addressed.

Emotionally immature parents sounds like a contradiction in terms, doesn't it? How could the gods of your early childhood not be mature? They were everything you knew about grown-ups. You were sheltered by them in a world entirely of their making. You modeled yourself after them, right down to your facial expressions and physical movements. For a long time, you thought they knew everything and held the sole right to judge your life. They punished you when you erred; they smiled on you when you were good. Their living example was your template for what to expect from life. You knew they loved you because they took care of you. You had no way of knowing that love is more than being cared for physically.

What makes coming to terms with parental immaturity confusing is that emotional immaturity can coexist with other adult capabilities. Despite developmental inadequacies in some areas, other areas of an EI parent's functioning—intellectual, social, occupational—can develop well. For instance, an EI parent might be an intellectual college professor or research scientist. They might be a highly successful businessperson. Or the EI parent could be socially adept, well respected, and popular in their social circles. But just because parents have grown up doesn't mean that they've matured. It's perfectly possible for you to be more emotionally mature than your parents.

EI parents can be highly responsible and self-sacrificing when it comes to putting bread on the table and to minding children's physical needs. Additionally, EI parents can be embedded in communities of like-minded people who support their values and behaviors. Their maturity would never be questioned because they fit in with the larger group's values and are appreciated by their peers and neighbors. This was the case with Tanya's parents, who were admired in their community, appeared to put family first, and gave time and money to their church.

But as well regarded as an EI parent can be, they may not be able to relate to you in a way that makes you feel connected and understood. Their emotional immaturity might only become noticeable when you need them emotionally, seeking tenderness or sensitivity to your feelings. With EI parents, you might grow up feeling *emotionally lonely*, unseen for who you are, and sad about not feeling quite good enough.

In contrast, sufficiently emotionally *mature* parents have developed enough individuality and self-awareness of their own that they grasp the truth that their children and other people have minds and feelings of their own. They see people as whole, dynamic individuals. Adequately emotionally mature parents are clear on their own values and reasoning, but they treat differing viewpoints respectfully. They consider others' feelings but protect their own well-being too. They reflect on their own behavior and take responsibility for their mistakes. Overall, adequately emotionally mature people have empathy for others, self-reflect, enjoy getting emotionally close to other people, and try to be objective about themselves and others. (For a further comparison of emotional maturity and immaturity, please see appendix B.)

Let's take a look at how you might sort out your feelings over your parent's possible emotional immaturity.

Strategy

Different parts of yourself may be in conflict over identifying your parents as emotionally immature. One part may acknowledge the evidence, while another part insists it's not true. Your job is to reconcile your feelings about this so you know where you stand. Our goal is not to be critical or disloyal toward these people, but to understand how they've affected you and where their reactions came from. Using a technique from internal family systems therapy (Schwartz 1995, 2022), let's try a dialogue between you and your conflicting parts.

Reflection and Self-Discovery

Ask the part of you that feels loyal and protective toward your parents: What are you afraid might happen if you viewed them as emotionally immature?

_____

_____

_____

Ask the part of you that feels hurt and confused by your parents—or that feels exasperated and angry with their behavior—if there's anything appealing about considering them emotionally immature?

_____

_____

_____

If both sides of you agree that you can still love and respect your parents as much as you want to, ask if each would willing to go forward and continue seeking a deeper understanding of its feelings?

_____

_____

Tip: You may realize that the protectiveness you feel toward your parents might be keeping you from realizing the truth of your own history. If you don't acknowledge the forces that impacted you in the past, you may be limited to living a reactive life instead of a created life. Processing your upbringing can help you have more genuine relationships, not only with other adults but especially with the children in your life as well.

3

Are both my parents immature?

Different types of EI parents

Sean's mother and father were different as night and day. Sean described his mother, Gina, as "hell on wheels," while his father, Levon, was "steady as a rock." While Sean's mother became overwhelmed and volatile whenever something unexpected happened, his father chugged along, taking everything in stride. After Gina blew up and cursed at the kids, Levon would come in their room and explain that their mother was super-stressed and needed their patience. "She doesn't really mean it," he would say. Sean had warm memories of close times with his dad, and he admired the way he got up every day and went to a job he didn't like just to give them financial stability. However, Levon drank too much, and although he was comforting at times, he never stepped in to protect the kids when Gina was out of control.

While Gina was obviously an emotionally immature parent, Levon was harder to peg. Sean didn't think Levon was emotionally immature because he had been empathic toward the kids and not mean like Gina. However, Levon didn't protect them, and he only supported them when he wasn't in Gina's line of fire. While Levon lacked Gina's volatility, he was impulsive in his own way, drinking himself to sleep every evening. Levon showed passive emotional immaturity, while Gina's immature behavior was active and forceful.

Emotional immaturity covers a range of personality styles. Characteristics of immaturity may be found in many personality disorders and symptom syndromes, as well as in people who have never been psychologically diagnosed. Emotional immaturity is its own condition, a particular way of being in the world that carries unique repercussions for EIPs and those around them.

There are four types of EI parent: emotional, driven, rejecting, and passive. EI parents of the first three types are more *active* in the way they control situations, while the *passive* type tends to be more good-natured, avoiding conflict and camouflaging their egocentricity. Parents can be more than one of these types, but usually they fit one best.

Emotional. Gina was an *emotional* type of EI parent. She had low stress tolerance and erupted whenever her limited self-control was challenged. Gina made a virtue of necessity, claiming

she was just being honest when she yelled her feelings. Swearing at the kids didn't mean anything because she just "lost her temper" because they'd been "testing" her all day. She complained that Levon was too soft on the kids, but she seemed relieved when he was dealing
with them. Of all the types, emotional EI parents are most likely to be diagnosed with psychological symptoms, such as personality disorders, post-traumatic stress disorder (PTSD), depression, or anxiety. Children of this parental type may fear and worry about their parent and
respond to their volatile behavior by being extra good, becoming withdrawn, or leaving the
family altogether.

Driven. This type of EI parent may seem mature and capable because they are so busy and
successful. They are driven to stay active, accomplish things, and be noticed. Usually perfectionistic, they love to take over and improve things—including their children. If you are the
child of a driven EI parent, you may have been well cared for and provided advantages and
activities, but you might have also felt pushed to do more than you wanted to or felt judged
for not doing enough. You may have felt like a nuisance when you needed your parent's attention, as if your needs were unnecessary interruptions to their pressing pursuits.

Driven parents may schedule activities to the point that their children feel simultaneously
overscheduled and overlooked. Such parents lack the tenderness and emotional connection
that make a child feel safe to open up about feelings. It's hard for these parents to slow down
and be present with an upset child; they avoid emotional intimacy and head right into problem
solving.

Rejecting. Rejecting EI parents have little interest in their children and prefer to be left alone.
As a child of a rejecting EI parent, you may have experienced a remote coldness that made
you feel unwelcome and unloved. These parents may support the family and provide for their
children's physical needs, but they leave affection and interaction for someone else to handle,
if they think of these things at all. They just don't see why that should be their problem. Some
of them are gruff and taciturn, others aloof and superior, but they all keep their distance and
get angry if they're intruded upon. Rejecting parents are dominant EI types even if they don't
say much because they forcefully communicate negativity and resentment while actively
repelling people with their demeanor.

Passive. Passive parents, like Levon, are the least likely to be recognized as emotionally immature. They are the good-natured parents who seem to like children and to enjoy being with
them. They are more tenderhearted than the other types, less hostile, and can be more fun

loving. Usually, they are the favorite parent, and the children feel closest to them. They avoid conflict and typically give in to more forceful types.

Even though they are nicer, passive parents don't necessarily notice how things affect their children emotionally. For instance, they may show superficial sympathy but be unable to really understand and resonate with their child's deeper feelings. They may seem more open and warmer, but when it comes to real emotional connection they remain focused on themselves. Their immaturity shows itself in the self-centeredness of their decision making, and they can be oblivious to their behavior's negative impact on their children. For instance, when they've had enough of a bad relationship, they might leave without thinking much about the kids.

Passive EI parents may seem more stable, loving, and fun than the other types, but when it comes to protecting their kids, their passivity allows their children to suffer. The most negative quality of these parents is their unwillingness to shield their children from aggressive, authoritarian, or mentally ill personalities. For example, they might turn a blind eye to harsh punishments or child abuse by their spouse. Passive parents often rationalize the other parent's behavior, believing they didn't intend to be so harmful. In this way, they teach their children to make excuses for other people's loss of control or mistreatment.

If you had a passive EI parent, you may have identified the actively immature parent as the problem and only much later realized how much the passive parent let you down. Often adult children of emotionally immature parents (ACEIPs) are so grateful for the passive parent's attention that they don't notice they weren't adequately protected. Anger at passive parents can be late in coming, but it's crucial to explore it.

You may wonder if nicer, less negative passive parents are more mature than the other types. Family systems therapist Murray Bowen (1978) believed that people tend to marry a partner who has about the same level of emotional maturity, or "level of differentiation" as he called it. He said that even if one partner seems to be more problematic, the other partner is likely to be similarly emotionally immature. However, there are many reasons—such as environments, circumstances, and cultures—why two people with mismatched levels of emotional maturity might end up with children together. Nevertheless, such partnerships may not last due to the disparities in maturity. As Bowen noted, people who differ in emotional maturity even a little tend to find each other incompatible.

Let's look at how categorizing the emotional immaturity of your parents—and perhaps others—can empower you.

Strategy

Because mythic-role labels like "parent" carry cultural power, thinking about and naming your parents' behavioral type can help free you from seeing them as irreproachable and infallible authority figures. When you can assess difficult people, you see them more realistically, and they lose some of their power over you. When you're able to classify something, you become less intimidated.

Reflection and Discovery

Which style of emotional immaturity—or mixtures of styles—did each of your parents exhibit?

_____

_____

_____

_____

What might you say to each parent about how their particular style affected you growing up?

_____

_____

_____

_____

Tip: Words make us think clearly. Labeling someone's behaviors engages your mind and pauses your emotional reactions. If you observe and name their behavior, you won't be as likely to internalize or imitate it. A more accurate label lets you question what previously seemed normal and gives you a chance to assess its effect on you.

4

Why do they act like that?

Spotting immature coping styles and defenses

Mehmet's mother, Esma, was the emotional type of EI parent. Mehmet had long felt drained by Esma's moods and emotional dependency. Mehmet's father had left when he was young, and his mother complained to Mehmet endlessly about his father's abandonment and irresponsibility. Mehmet had tried to tell her how uncomfortable it made him, but she dismissed his feelings. He hated hearing his father criticized yet felt he needed to be there for his mother because she was always so unhappy. When Mehmet got married, he and his wife stayed close to his mother, living in the same apartment building.

Instead of being grateful that her son was nearby, Esma complained about how little time he now had for her. She wanted to be included in the new couple's activities and expected them to do all the inviting. When Mehmet finally set limits on her involvement, she accused him of abandoning her, too, told him to just forget about her, and accused his wife of turning him against her. Some days she refused to answer his texts until he felt he had to physically go and check on her. Mehmet could do nothing right, and nothing he did was ever enough. Yet he had been a devoted son. Why was she acting like this?

Objectively, this makes no sense at all. Somehow Esma had succeeded in making Mehmet feel guilty for being a normal adult. He had been nothing but loyal to her and yet she cast him as another villain in her life. Her antagonism was palpable, yet she hid behind her woundedness like a victim, making it seem cruel to confront her. If he ever criticized her, she told him she was being a good mother, just like her mother, and he should be a good son.

Esma was proving the rule that many EIPs are extremely defensive people, with most interactions centered around keeping the power balance in their favor. Their psychological defenses, or coping mechanisms, automatically jump in to protect them at the first hint of anxiety or insecurity (S. Freud 1894; Schwartz 1995, 2022). These defenses are automatic, unintentional, involuntary, and unconscious. Anything that arouses their anxiety can activate the kind of hair-trigger defenses that Mehmet's mother showed.

EIP's coping mechanisms stay immature (G. Vaillant 1977, 2000) because, instead of sizing up changing circumstances—and adjusting their responses accordingly—they deny, dismiss, or distort reality according to how they feel. Like children, EIPs believe their viewpoint is right no matter what. Also, parents may show EI behavior because it was culturally sanctioned in their families. Like Esma, many EI parents model themselves (Bandura 1971) after their parents, with no thought for how it's affecting their children.

EIPs see their relationships in a fused, undifferentiated way (Bowen 1978). For them, families and relationships are not connections between autonomous individuals but a meld of shared selves and identities. EIPs like Esma don't experience loved ones as different or separate from them. They expect others to know what they need and to give it to them, even at the cost of their own selfhood. If the loved one asserts their independent self, it could only mean that they don't love the EIP. Why else would they pull away or need space for themselves? EIPs certainly feel no urge for psychological independence. For them, psychological fusion is how loving relationships should be—a perfectly healthy belief for a toddler, but not for an adult. As for Mehmet, he wished he could have an authentic relationship with his mother in which he didn't fear saying no to her.

Because adult EIPs are verbal, they seem more capable of mature reasoning than they really are. As with four-year-olds, EIPs are frustrating because their verbal ability makes you think they can be reasoned with, but their immaturity makes them reactive and stubborn. They can talk and reason up to the point where they want something. Then they dig in their heels on their demands.

Projection is a favorite EI defense; instead of feeling bad about themselves, EIPs blame others for their own failings (A. Freud 1936). Esma blamed Mehmet for abandoning her while she was the one who had emotionally deserted him for years, showing no concern for having put him in the middle of her relationship with his father. She accused Mehmet of heartlessness, yet she was the one who was unmoved by his pleas not to dump her emotional pain onto him.

Esma also projected her egocentrism on Mehmet, seeing him as selfish. Mehmet couldn't please his mother because her suspiciousness rendered her unable to recognize love or be nurtured by it. She kept her guard up, always looking for the snake in the basket. Perhaps childhood traumas had made her that way, but that didn't make it any easier on Mehmet. She focused on her anger and wounded pride no matter how hard he tried. Mehmet eventually stopped feeling guilty for having his own life and refused to agree with Esma that his independence was an unloving act. In his words, "You can keep your personhood and be a loving person too."

When they are caught up in defensiveness, EIPs are unreachable. They are the victim; you are the villain. They won't listen to reason and have no empathy for your point of view. You may be dumbfounded as they irrationally stick to their positions. For EIPs, lowering their defenses and being accountable for their behavior feels unimaginable. For them, admitting fault is tantamount to baring their throat to the enemy.

Now let's take a look at how you can disentangle from EI defensiveness while remaining centered and self-confident.

Strategy

It's important for you to see through an EIP's defenses, distortions, and projective coping style. You will feel far less confused and guilty if you do. Notice how they use guilt, shame, fear, and self-doubt to emotionally coerce you. Don't take the blame if it doesn't make sense. Tune in to your view of the truth and don't be maneuvered out of your reality.

Remember that EIPs deny, dismiss, or distort reality. You can't talk them out of their defensive position. The more you try to get them to be rational, the more frustrated you will become. What can you do instead? Try accepting their right to see it their way, but without feeling you have to accept their distortions. Your only job is to decide what *you're* going to do next, regardless of whether you see eye to eye. Silently label their defensive behavior and resist the urge to argue. Instead, make your choices based on what's best for you, inform them of your decisions, and repeat as necessary. You're a fellow adult. You don't need their buy-in or approval.

Reflection and Discovery

You can break a pattern if you see it coming. Which of the following EI defenses makes you feel most unsure of yourself? (Check as many as apply.)

- ☐ They imply you are mean or selfish for not doing what they want.
- ☐ They imply you have a moral obligation to put their needs first.
- ☐ They flat out deny what they did or that something happened.
- ☐ They act like you have wounded them by confronting them.
- ☐ They dismiss your concern as ridiculous or unimportant.
- ☐ They accuse you of being out to get them.
- ☐ They claim things that are blatantly untrue.

Determine which ploys work best on you so you can be ready the next time they use them.

Write your EIP an *unsent* letter in your journal telling them how you feel about them holding you responsible for their unhappiness.

Tip: The defensiveness of EIPs can make you question reality. Most of us don't understand why people would warp reality so much. Perhaps they do it for the same reason children tell lies, even if they're sure to be caught: It makes them momentarily feel better. It gives them an immediate advantage and makes them feel justified. Their motive is all about escaping anxiety in the moment, with no thought of future repercussions. If you accept that, it all makes sense. Deep down, you know what reality is. That's all that matters.

5

They are so contradictory; it baffles me.

Why EIPs are inconsistent and extreme

Jim finally had enough of his father Dan's bullying behavior. Jim told his father that he couldn't visit again until they talked honestly about how Dan had hurt and demeaned him over the years. Dan claimed to have no idea what Jim was talking about and denied that he had ever been anything but proud of him. However, he said he was willing to do anything Jim wanted to put things right. But when Jim requested a phone conversation, his father insisted on talking in person on his next visit. Jim reminded him there would be no next visit until they talked. Dan blew up, as if this was totally unexpected, and told him he had been a good father and didn't want to hear a bunch of nonsense otherwise. Jim was dumbfounded and briefly questioned his own sanity: Hadn't they agreed to talk? Hadn't his father said he wanted to put things right?

It wasn't just that Dan had changed his mind; it was that Dan made up his own version of their conversation and asserted a view of reality that Jim knew wasn't true.

For EIPs, as soon as emotions get involved, truth doesn't get in the way of their opinion. Dan's contradictoriness showed his utter lack of concern over being inconsistent, which is common in EIPs. People like this don't have multiple personalities, but they're not cohesive people either. Their personalities are poorly integrated, allowing them to engage in behaviors that contradict each other. They focus on the part that interests them now and ignore the whole picture. That is why they can tell you one thing, and then later claim something completely different.

Although EIPs are inconsistent, they seem utterly sincere in the moment. This is what makes them so convincing when they flip-flop later. But the part of them that you form a relationship with *now* may not be the same part you have to deal with *later*. As you can imagine, their capacity for hypocrisy is enormous.

In contrast, an adequately emotionally mature person experiences an intact sense of self across time, linking their experiences to form their life memory, like adding beads to a string. Their durable sense of self is the string connecting all their experiences, with new moments being added to and organized alongside the rest of their life storyline. Sufficiently emotionally mature people have a continuous, unitary self-awareness across time, making it uncomfortable for them to say one thing and then do another. As a result, their personalities are integrated and consistent.

But the bits of an EIP's self-memories are like pearls scattered in a cardboard box; they freely roll around unattached to the others. For EIPs, each significant experience forms a stand-alone, separate emotional memory, some good, some bad (Kernberg 1975). But there's no unifying sense of self-continuity binding their experiences together across time. That's what allows EIPs to be so stunningly contradictory in their behaviors. When their actions are at odds with who they've been, it doesn't bother them because their past and present aren't meaningfully related. They don't see the discrepancy, why it matters, or why you're upset by it. They don't feel internal conflict because there isn't enough psychological integration among their emotional memories to make the mismatch uncomfortable.

EIPs may be affectionate and fun one minute and raging at you the next. But because they inhabit one "pearl" moment at a time, they don't register the contradiction. To them, their immediate mood is totally justified and disconnected from the past or future. Remember, their *feelings* determine their reality, so reality, like their sense of self, is malleable. It changes and shifts with each new feeling. Without a reliable sense of self or the capacity for self-reflection, EIPs don't experience *cognitive dissonance* (Festinger 1957) about their behavior, that uneasy discomfort you feel when you hold two beliefs that seem mutually exclusive. For example, many EIPs wouldn't be bothered by professing one thing and doing something else, as long as nobody called them on it.

If you have an integrated personality with a unified sense of self and personal experience, you hate to go back on your word, lie to someone's face, or avoid problems by blaming someone else. But without *integrity*—literally an integrated self—an EIP isn't bothered by such inconsistency. EIPs with low integrity are not bound by the same concern for reality or consistency that keeps a person from betraying their values or other people for an expedient gain. Integrity is meaningless when your highest good lies in your immediate advantage of the moment. Integrity can't be sustained in a person who privileges their feelings over factual reality.

If you are an internalizer type of ACEIP, you probably have adequate integrity and inner consolidation. This is because internalizers, from an early age, try to understand and integrate their experiences, making them fit together (see chapter 11). Internalizers feel embarrassed if someone points out an inconsistency because the inconsistency feels like a betrayal of self. It is therefore maddening when an EIP flatly denies something they did or said, implying there's something wrong with you for even mentioning it.

Since EIPs are guided by their immediate emotional experience, they ignore long-term future effects and cause-and-effect timelines. They can tell time, of course—a different part of the brain orients us to clocks, schedules, and deadlines—but they lack the empathy and emotional imagination to anticipate the future impact of their actions on other people.

Many ACEIPs try to get EIPs to understand how their inconsistent behavior makes them feel. But this is asking for a level of empathy and mentalization that they don't have. EIPs don't think about their behavior's impact because, as it is for a small child, future consequences seem emotionally unreal. That's why it's so hard for them to wait, delay gratification, or resist a self-serving lie. For you, if you're an internalizer, your imagined future may feel almost as real as the present, so it's easier to be patient. When you think of how something might feel tomorrow, your imaginative leap makes it very real. You experience that internal timeline of cause and effect. They don't.

EIP's lack of emotional- and self-continuity means they won't understand why you are still upset about something they did last week or last year. They have already moved on to a different pearl in the box. They don't feel empathy for what they see as "wallowing" in the past. *Why can't you see that was then, and this is now?* They expect immediate forgiveness and are frustrated and offended when their apology doesn't make everything right again. They don't want to learn or improve themselves; they want you to stop. Not experiencing self-continuity across time, they can't understand why other people remain upset with them—and will be for quite a while.

You can see how this lack of psychological integration could create future problems for EIPs. They frequently experience consequences they did not anticipate. When a person lives in separate, disconnected states inside, they are always surprised in the long run. Distressing things happen to EIPs and they think it's bad luck, fate, or other people, when the real problem is their lack of adequate anticipation.

Let's think about how you might deal with this EI inconsistency.

Strategy

Instead of being outraged in disbelief at their denial or switch ups, what if you *expected* them to do contradictory things? See them as that three-year-old with chocolate on their face who denies they ate the cake. What if you ignored their self-justifications and calmly restated your request or boundary? You don't let them off the hook, but you don't let them make you miserable either. You remind yourself that this is what they do. You stop trying to change how their brain works. You use their behavior to inform how much to trust them later. How might that feel?

Reflection and Discovery

Write about a time when you experienced an EIP's inconsistency. How did you feel and react?

_____

_____

_____

_____

_____

_____

Now imagine that you are fully aware of why they are so inconsistent. Write them an unsent letter in your journal about how you now understand their puzzling behavior.

Tip: If you want a relationship with an EIP, the best way to cope is to become complex enough within yourself to be able to recognize and label their inconsistencies without banging your head against the wall. As you learn how to predict and maneuver around them, their contradictory positions become just part of the landscape to be traversed.

6

Why is it always about them?

How EIPs see the world

Lara was in a constant state of emotional overload. Although she handled her responsibilities as a mother with care and sensitivity, she always felt one jump ahead of panic. Her two active little boys were always getting scraped up or worse, and their normal childhood illnesses terrified her. Lara handled everything well; her coping was impeccable, but on the inside she felt like an abandoned seven-year-old responsible for younger children in a home with no adults. She figured things out but never felt confident about her decisions.

It was no wonder Lara was chronically anxious despite her excellent problem solving. Lara's mother had been an intensely reactive, angry woman who was preoccupied with her own childhood traumas. She was chronically belligerent because everything reminded her of a betrayal from childhood. Lara's mother often accused her of trying to drive her crazy, just like her mother's sister used to. If her mother got worried about finances, she threw the whole household into turmoil by cursing her husband for being lazy like her father. Everything was a rerun of her mother's childhood issues, as if her whole family were conspiring to re-create her miserable childhood.

When Lara went to her mother with a problem, her mother accused her of trying to make her life harder. If Lara talked about relationship worries, her mother topped it with stories of her own. Clearly, Lara's mother saw herself as the most important person in the family. As Lara put it, "Why was it always all about her?"

Growing up with little empathy or comfort from her mother, it's no wonder Lara felt overwhelmed when problems hit. Feeling she had to do everything right, Lara scrutinized her reactions in a way that intensified her anxiety. Now as a mother herself, she felt all alone with her worries, overwhelmed by the responsibility of it all. Her aloneness reflected her experience growing up with a self-preoccupied mother who couldn't see that her daughter needed help too.

Lara's mother, like all EIPs, viewed the world egocentrically through her emotions. Similar to young children, EIPs aren't psychologically mature enough to conceptualize someone else's experience or empathize with them. EIPs are stranded on that young developmental plateau where they're only attentive to their own experiences.

Lara's mother was an extremely toxic example of this; other more benign EI parents might direct attention back to themselves in a more pleasant manner ("That reminds me of when…"), but the egocentrism is the same. We become interested in others because someone has been interested in us. When loved ones show curiosity about our subjective experience, we learn to extend that same curiosity to others. We learn that it's important to show interest in others, and we learn how to hold a conversation.

EIPs may not have been so lucky. Perhaps they grew up with a minimum of adult attentiveness to their inner experiences. They may have come from a family in which a child's feelings and needs took a back seat to survival or economic issues. Or they may have grown up in a culture that condemned individuality unless one was an authority figure. Such children never learned to be social in ways that recognize other people. Instead, the prize of reaching adulthood for these EIPs might have felt like the right to expect others to put *them* in the spotlight. For such a child, growing up meant finally being able to make everything about them.

Some self-centered EIPs may have had the opposite problem. Maybe they were given a privileged role in their family; they were treated as very special to the point that their parent didn't rein in their natural childhood grandiosity enough to socialize them. Such permissiveness may sound like unconditional love, but this harmful leniency binds the child tightly to the parent and deprives them of learning to consider other people. Self-involved parents who don't teach their children how to think of others are projecting their own sense of narcissistic privilege onto that child. The child's identity becomes inflated as they enmesh with the parents' sense of entitlement to an unhealthy degree. These future EIPs grow up assuming that all attention should continue to be on them. Other people's feelings and needs just don't register. Their gratification is all that matters.

Can you think of a time when an EIP derailed your attempt to tell them something by taking over and acting like it was all about them? Let's consider how best to respond to such situations.

Strategy

If you don't have a reasonably healthy acceptance of your own basic rights, you may fall into making it all about the EIP. The first step to changing this dynamic is to claim your following basic rights (see the "Bill of Rights" in appendix D):

- I have the right to be considered just as important as you.

- I have the right to speak up and tell you what I really prefer.

- I have the right to stay away from anyone who is unpleasant or draining.

If you incorporate these rights into your thinking, it will be much easier to either steer self-absorbed conversations toward something you would rather discuss, or to politely bring the interaction to a close. When you become even more comfortable with yourself, you might break in and tell the EIP that now that you've heard their stories, you'd love to share one with them or see if there are other things you might have in common. Be ready with some conversation starters that will redirect them from their favorite takeover topics.

Reflection and Discovery

Recall a time you sought sympathy and understanding for a problem, and an EIP turned the topic back to themself. Describe how you felt and reacted.

_____

_____

_____

_____

_____

_____

_____

Describe how it might feel to ask an EIP to hold on and let you finish because there's more you want to tell them. By being proactive, perhaps you could avoid getting angry or exasperated.

_____

_____

_____

_____

_____

_____

Tip: EIPs expect you to accept that they are the most important person in the interaction. You are assigned a supporting role, to help them live out their agendas. It's up to you to address this inequity and lack of reciprocity by claiming your right to attention as well. Passive listening only adds to your exhaustion, never to mutually beneficial communication. Remember, your interests and needs are just as important as theirs.

Nothing I do is ever enough.

Why nothing makes EIPs happy for long

EIPs seem to have trouble enjoying happiness once they get it. It may be human nature to keep wanting more, but it's emotional immaturity when a person can't feel satisfaction or appreciation for what they're given.

Adequately mature people feel gratitude when someone tries to help them or give them something. They may or may not want what the other person offers, but they notice the generous intent and it makes them feel cared about. In turn, they express thanks and appreciation, completing a little cycle of pleasant connection. Everybody feels good after such an exchange. It is enjoyable to help these people because you feel acknowledged and good about what you've done.

Unfortunately, it's unsatisfying to give to EIPs because they often act like whatever you do is not enough. They might brighten momentarily, but the reaction quickly fades. You end up feeling like you've missed the mark, as if you didn't guess what they really wanted. Trying to encourage them or give help feels like pouring water through a sieve; nothing is retained. Psychologist Leigh McCullough Vaillant (1997) calls this behavior poor "receptive capacity," and it's very common in people with rigid and immature coping styles. Unable to emotionally accept what you offer them, they leave you feeling frustrated and inadequate.

Depressed or easily angered EI parents, in particular, put their children in a bind. Children are unequipped to fix the mood of an unhappy adult, but most of them will try. When children aren't able to change their parent's mood for the better, they feel defeated. Their EI parent's continuing dissatisfaction is demoralizing; they are burdened with the feeling that they have not tried hard enough. Children take their parents' emotional fluctuations personally because they secretly feel responsible for how their parents treat them.

Adequately mature parents may get depressed or angry, too, but they usually don't convey the attitude that it's the child's fault or that they've been wronged by a lack of caring. Even if they're not cheered up by their child's attempts to make them feel better, they're empathic enough to appreciate the effort.

Sometimes upset EI parents strike at the heart of their children's sense of worth, suggesting that the child themself is not enough. Such a parent makes their child feel like no matter how hard they try, their parent is unimpressed. This can affect the child's self-esteem all their life, leaving them feeling like they must always try hard to qualify for love, regard, and support.

One man I worked with was terrified to start dating after his divorce. He never felt he looked nice enough or drove a good enough car to impress his date. When he met someone new, he worked hard to be entertaining, witty, and a "catch" in order to get a second date. He soon dreaded going out because it was so utterly exhausting. When I asked what it would be like if he stopped trying so hard, he said he was sure that unless he put on this show, his date would assess him as simply "not enough." (This had actually been true with his very critical mother.)

In childhood, an EI parent's poor receptive capacity can warp your future opinion of your own generosity and altruism. We learn to enjoy generosity when others react appreciatively to our giving; their warm feedback encourages our altruistic impulses. But if your depressed or disgruntled parent continually signaled that you missed the mark—or didn't care enough, or care in the right way—you may end up feeling inadequate and relationally inept in adulthood. When you give it your all and your loved one still seems unhappy, you may conclude that there must be something missing in you. It wouldn't occur to you that your feeling was rooted in growing up with a parent who had problems with receiving love.

Why do EIPs have trouble receiving love?

Perhaps your EIP or EI parent had disturbing early attachment experiences with their own parents. In the maternal separation research by Ainsworth, Bell, and Stayton (1974), some very young children were observed to act as if their mothers were unreliable or emotionally untrustworthy. These children reacted to brief separations as if abandoned, but then seemed ambivalent when their mothers returned to care for them. The children sought comfort from the mother, but then seemed angry or dissatisfied with what the mother gave. The mother was called upon to nurture, but then was pushed away when she tried. Such a situation can spiral downward if the mother, too, feels rejected and loses confidence in her ability to satisfy her child. She might even believe the child doesn't like her, or that she is no good as a mother.

Such insecurity and ambivalence on the mother's part makes an already difficult situation worse. Just when the situation calls for the mother to show more sensitivity and perseverance to make the connection, she either defensively pulls back or forces her overtures on the child. When children feel their primary caretaker is out of synch with their emotional state, it can negatively affect that child's receptive capacity in future relationships.

So how should you respond when an EI parent—or EIP in general—seems dissatisfied no matter what you do?

Strategy

First, remain empathetic to yourself. Feel the normal hurt and disappointment that occurs when others reject your caring. But before you move into anger, pull back and ask yourself what you're trying to do in your interaction. If it has anything to do with making them happy, pull back even further to revisit your motivation and adjust if necessary. Remind yourself that you *are* loving and giving, but that they can't enjoy this kind of caring with you. It's unsatisfying and deflating, but you did your part, and then some. It's not up to you to force them into joy; they would have found it already if they could.

Reflection and Discovery

Describe a time when you tried to make an EI loved one feel better and you came away feeling inadequate, as if you had failed to give them enough.

Write down privately what you'd like to tell them about no longer taking responsibility for their happiness. Put it in your own words, but get it across that you're no longer investing energy in their poor receptive capacity.

_____

_____

_____

_____

_____

_____

_____

Tip: You can offer the help that you want to, but don't give until it hurts. Self-sacrifice is not a healthy goal. You never owe anybody a do-over of their unhappy childhood. If you feel that you honestly tried to help or show love, don't let the EIP's discontent make you doubt yourself. You know if you tried to help or be supportive. No EIP gets to define that for you.

8

Why is it so hard to get close or share anything real with them?

Why EIPs shut down emotional intimacy

Brandy longed for a mother who would sit down beside her and listen to her when she had a problem. But Brandy's mother, Rose, had always seemed uncomfortable when Brandy confided in her. Sometimes she would tell Brandy not to worry or flippantly offer useless retorts ("You should just tell them that…"). Sometimes Rose would interrupt with unsolicited advice, but most of the time Rose seemed impatient or changed the subject to herself ("You think you have problems… Let me tell you what happened to me!"). Brandy never felt Rose's interest, but she thought it was her fault for failing to hold her mother's attention. Brandy figured she was too needy and overly sensitive. As a result, she felt shy and embarrassed about telling anyone what was really going on with her, certain that they would quickly tire of her.

Sharing emotional intimacy and deep feelings makes EIPs nervous. Dominant EI types will shut down your emotions one way or another, while more passive EIPs may ignore or placate you. But both types prefer shallow communication, focusing on trivialities, gossip (often about people you don't know well), their interests, or events. Their superficiality gives off the clear message that they have no interest in relating at a deeper level. Attempts to talk about something meaningful might bring a chitchat brush-off ("Don't be silly!") or dismissive denials ("No, you're not!" "That's not true!"). Whatever their response, you end up feeling invalidated. If, like Brandy, you grew up with EI parents who did this, it can be hard to imagine that others could be interested in your thoughts and feelings.

Discounting other people's feelings is poisonous to long-term bonds and marriages, not to mention the relationship between parent and child. When a person won't discuss feelings (or other meaningful topics), it creates tension in the relationship and isolates us in emotional loneliness. We all feel better when someone takes our feelings seriously, shows concern, and offers us comfort. It's strengthening to get eye contact, full attention, warm responses, and reassuring physical touch (Porges 2017). Being validated by others is an important source of our resilience as human beings.

However, deep, authentic interactions frighten EIPs, making them feel nervous and overwhelmed. They avoid emotional vulnerability because they've never learned how to feel deeply without becoming destabilized. Even kinder, gentler EIPs will back up if you show too much feeling. They don't know what to do with someone who bares their soul in a desire to be understood. Instead of addressing your emotions, the EIP may try to talk you out of them—anything to shut down the emotional intensity. They've rarely experienced this kind of intimacy themselves, so they don't know how it's done or even why it's done.

Instead of talking to you directly about feelings, EIPs are more likely to entice another person into talking about you behind your back. They would rather talk *about* you rather than talk *to* you. This *triangulation* (Bowen 1978) with another person creates a momentary sense of intimacy with their confidant, although these alliances tend to be shaky and insincere. Triangulation is like the friendship politics of a third-grader: we're on the same side if we can label someone else as the outsider.

Nevertheless, there are some clever EIPs who can go straight into deep topics and be very insightful about your motives and feelings. They create a rapid intimacy, and their laser-like interest can make you feel dazzled and deeply understood. (Cult leaders are very skilled at this.) Yet over time you will notice that such a person doesn't process their emotional experiences with you in a reciprocal way. Instead of a mutual sharing between equals, the relationship feels one-sided. Rather than offering true friendship, they're giving you a performance. You are the object of their charm offensive rather than someone to whom they're genuinely relating.

What can you do when an EIP keeps evading your attempts at mutual closeness and communication?

Strategy

Maybe the EIP in question won't initiate real communication, but what if *you* experimented with sharing some feelings in slightly more meaningful ways? You could start by asking if they would listen to you for just ten minutes, setting up a mini-foundation for a more meaningful interaction. If the person agrees but breaks in with advice or quips, ask them to just listen for a few more minutes, explaining to them that it's incredibly nice just to be listened to. When your ten minutes is up, thank them for listening so well and tell them how much you enjoyed talking to them. Ask if they want to tell you anything, but if they don't, that can be the end of the interaction.

EIPs have no repertoire of behavior for how to make other people feel truly listened to and cared about. You literally may have to educate them about the basics of emotional communication. This won't be particularly satisfying for you, but it will give you practice in speaking up for what you need. I don't recommend using this strategy frequently; it can get too frustrating. But once in a while you can use it to explicitly guide an EIP to give you more of what you need. Even if they don't change much, you can feel good about your own honesty and directness. Give them details of the kind of responses you'd like. Don't wait for them to figure out something they have no experience with.

Reflection and Discovery

How do you feel when an EIP won't listen to you with any depth?

_____

_____

What do you typically do when this EIP doesn't show interest? Do you become disappointed and withdraw? Get angry? Write about your typical response. Is it passive and resentful? Or active and self-affirming?

_____

_____

_____

_____

Tip: If the EIP refuses more meaningful communication, why not back off and use the time to listen to yourself instead? Journaling about how you feel will bring you closer to yourself by putting your experiences into words. Write about your experience, exactly what you wished for from them, and how it felt to be kept at a superficial level. Your journal gives you a listening ear when you need it, plus it helps you process your thoughts and feelings at a deeper level.

9

Why do they make it so hard to want to be around them?

Why EI behavior makes you need to get away

Mandy had a happy homelife with her husband, Jack, and their three children, but she dreaded visits from her parents. Mandy's father, Frank, was a stern, judgmental man and successful small-business owner. He didn't approve of Mandy's choice of Jack, a musician, and couldn't imagine what she saw in him. He made Mandy feel self-conscious about their small home and repeatedly gave Jack unwanted advice on how to make more money. If something offended Frank during their visits, the whole family was expected to walk on eggshells until he was in a better mood. Nothing ever seemed to be done well enough to please him.

Mandy's mother, Pam, on the other hand, was a passive counterpoint to her husband's moodiness and entitlement. She made excuses for him, waited on him, and adopted a falsely bright demeanor as she chatted about superficial news from home. She liked to cook and play games with Mandy's children but seemed at a loss when they needed comforting. She frequently sent the kids presents, but they seemed to be chosen without their interests in mind. During visits, if Mandy attempted to talk with her mother about a problem she was having, Pam would pat Mandy's hand and assure her she would figure it out. Mandy just couldn't get beneath the surface of her mother's personality.

Although Mandy's parents were opposite personalities, they each had the hallmarks of emotional immaturity. They both lacked empathy, were self-preoccupied, and avoided emotional intimacy. In addition to their lack of empathy, they also had trouble *mentalizing* (Fonagy and Target 2008) other people's inner experiences: in addition to not tuning in to Mandy's feelings, they couldn't imagine or appreciate what might be going on in her *mind*.

Mandy and her parents were at different levels of emotional maturity and psychological individuation. As Murray Bowen (1978) described in family systems theory, emotionally immature family members seek psychological *fusion* with others in what he called the "undifferentiated family ego mass." In this state, people manage their anxieties by being overly involved with each other's lives and by projecting their issues onto each other. This overly "close" family fusion is what an ACEIP like Mandy wants to escape. Mandy sought what

Bowen called "differentiation" from her family, the right to become her own person instead of making family membership the highest good. On Bowen's differentiation scale of how well individuals have developed their individual identity, Mandy and her parents were far apart. Let's now look at the specific EI characteristics that made Mandy's parents difficult for her to be around.

Like most EIPs, Frank and Pam naturally assumed that as their daughter—in their minds, an extension of themselves—Mandy would want to be just like them. They didn't try to get to know Mandy as an adult, or her husband and kids, because they already had assumptions about them. Frank had no curiosity about Jack's life as a musician, and it didn't occur to Pam to ask the kids what they liked before she bought their gifts; she just bought them what she thought "children" would like. Both Frank and Pam ignored what was going on *inside* their child and grandchildren and instead expected them to like what they liked. They just assumed that being family means preferences are shared. With EIPs, you end up feeling like more of a prop in their life rather than a real person in their eyes.

Mandy's parents were also hard to be around because they expected to be in control. EIPs psychologically control you by pulling you into their *emotionally immature relationship system*, making you feel you should self-sacrifice to shore up their *emotional stability* and *self-esteem*. The need for this degree of emotional support is normal in children but suggests immaturity in adults.

The anxiety, reactivity, and egocentrism of EIPs make it feel emotionally unsafe to interact with them. They rarely do the emotional work (Fraad 2008) necessary to keep relationships in a good emotional place, such as showing patience, speaking kindly, or finding a tactful way of talking about problems. They almost always leave the emotional work to someone else. This is another reason they can be draining to be around. Who enjoys tiptoeing around someone's ego and giving them lots of attention while never expecting them to reciprocate?

Interactions with EIPs can make you feel drained, bored, and lethargic but also hypervigilant. Like Mandy, you feel de-energized but tense at the same time. How can you enjoy someone who isn't interested in getting to know you, expects you to put them first, and becomes judgmental if you're honest about your own preferences?

It's also off-putting when EIPs try to dominate you by putting a moralistic spin on their requests. They righteously make meeting their needs seem like your moral obligation (Shaw 2014). For instance, Mandy's father didn't just express his opinions, he adopted an air of superior moral authority while doing so. Anyone who said no to him was a bad person. Domineering EIPs like Frank expect you to function as an extension of them, a mini-me.

In addition, EI relationship fusion is likely to pull you into a *drama triangle* (Karpman 1968) in which you get pulled in to play one of three possible roles: innocent victim, aggressive villain, or heroic rescuer. If you listen to an EIP's life story, you'll detect these roles over and over, played to themes of betrayal and disappointment. The implication is that if you don't jump in to be their rescuer, you're just another letdown in their life story of oppression. While drama triangles are entertaining in novels and film, in real life these roles feel restrictive and strangely boring.

Finally, there is another subset of EIPs who are particularly hard to be around, those with a sadistic streak. They like to make people uncomfortable: they enjoy popping your balloon, humiliating you, or even causing you pain or trauma. By undermining your joy and self-esteem, they promote insecurity and unsafety. It's hard to believe that people close to you could enjoy causing you distress, but again, it's not about you. They like the sense of power and invulnerability it gives them.

How do you handle EI behavior when you don't enjoy the time spent with EIPs but want to maintain contact?

Strategy

EI people can be hard to enjoy. Maintaining your individuality around them can require constant effort. You can experiment with shorter contacts to find a level of connection that will be tolerable for everyone, especially you. Honoring family or friendship bonds with EIPs often works best in smaller doses. Shorter visits help everyone to stay at their best, while longer contacts invite regression into polarities of fusion or resistance. Due to differing levels of differentiation, it's nobody's fault if you find it hard to want to be around EI friends and family members.

Reflection and Discovery

Think of someone in your life who has EI characteristics. What do they do that makes you feel uncomfortable or irritated after you're around them for a while?

_____

_____

_____

_____

Now close your eyes and imagine spending an hour with someone whom you enjoy being around. What makes that interaction different from the one with the EIP?

_____

_____

_____

_____

Tip: Having an understanding of incompatible levels of differentiation helps to explain why you want to get away from EIPs at times. Differing levels of maturity quickly create tension. If there's no meeting of the minds or any emotional connection felt, you don't have to feel guilty about pulling back. You just have different interests and widely differing levels of complexity. If this causes conflict, your relationship may be better served with less exposure to each other. But no matter how much time you spend with them, you'll feel better if you remain aware of your own individuality regardless of the pressures you feel to be who they want you to be.

Is there hope for a better relationship?

Can EIPs ever change?

If you've ever caught glimpses of an EIP's softer side, you may think there must be a way to create a more respectful, authentic relationship. No matter how they've treated you, you still hope that a closer relationship might be possible. The hope that this person will one day become more empathic and emotionally accessible is what I call a "healing fantasy." This fantasy motivates you to find some way to reach them emotionally, to finally forge a rewarding connection.

If you had an EI parent, you needed that fantasy so you could grow up as strong as possible. It was to your developmental advantage to hold on to the possibility that you and your parent would develop a closer connection. That hope may have been a long shot, but it was a vision that sustained you.

Your hope for a better relationship also may be based on past good times with an EIP in your life. Perhaps they weren't always defensive or critical. When they were feeling safe and relaxed, they may have shown you sensitivity and warmth. It's not that EI people don't have *any* empathy, it's that their psychological defense systems so easily eclipse their feelings for others.

Sometimes EIPs make briefly sincere efforts at relationship repair, such as the cold authoritarians who express regret on their deathbed, abusers who are ashamed of themselves, or absent parents who express genuine remorse. At these moments, their hearts peek through their EI armor. When EIPs do show genuine concern for their children, the children never forget it. So, if you've experienced an EIP's real caring, even one time, it makes sense that you would keep hoping for more.

Usually, however, EIP's defenses keep an iron grip on their emotional life, even if they'd like to be more open. Their chronic insecurity initiates their defenses at the first sign of anxiety. Your efforts to reach them are no match for their quick-draw defenses. Their emotional reactivity is involuntary and instantaneous, even if they don't intend to hurt you. They blow up, criticize, make demands, or withdraw love before they even know it.

So, can EIPs change? Well, maybe the question should be, can they change and *stay* that way? In other words, can they go back, revamp their personality structure, process their traumas, gain insight into their behavior, find ways to make amends, and do the hard work to overcome years of reflexive defensiveness and projection of blame? It's possible, but extremely difficult.

Some EI people do mellow with age, becoming less impulsive and more mature across their lifetime (G. Vaillant 1977), gaining coping strengths and wisdom. For example, rigid parents may transform into doting (and patient) grandparents. Released from the responsibility of parenthood, some grandparents open their hearts to grandchildren in a way they could never do with their own children. It all depends on the rigidity of the person's defenses and the lucky factors that might come their way, for it's equally likely that the EI characteristics of some people will get worse over their lifetime.

Moments of peace and harmony with EIPs do raise hopes that they could be more reasonable, rational, and receptive if only you handle them right. You become careful not to say or do anything that could make them defensive. You might adopt a pleasing persona around them, in hopes that your careful behavior will keep things on an even keel.

You also may feel optimistic about changing them because you've learned effective communication skills, negotiating tactics, and other ways to get along with difficult people. You may hope that your new skills could create more equal and authentic relationships with the EI people in your life.

If you have hope that an EIP in your life will change, or that you will succeed in pleasing them, you'll probably keep seeking that elusive closeness with them. You may not realize what all this subconscious effort is costing you in tension and vigilance, because over time it starts to feel natural. The healing fantasy says the miracle reunion is just over the horizon—even when it isn't. Sometimes you don't know why you keep trying, but your dedication to improving the relationship is unshakable.

Usually, however, EIPs remain in their self-involved position. Just because you've developed solid interpersonal skills, it doesn't mean that the EIP will respond or want to communicate at a deeper level. No matter how adept you become at communication, you still have to deal with their egocentric responses.

The relationship may seem worth it to you even if it looks excruciating to outsiders. Human bonds run deep. With their empathy and sensitivity, ACEIPs hate to give up on anyone. But sometimes they reach a point where they need to disengage because the cost of maintaining connection is far too high, such as when the EIP becomes abusive, is excessively demanding, refuses to respect boundaries, or keeps taking over (such as by pushing advice or being controlling).

So, can an EIP change? It's not impossible, but it's unlikely as long as they refuse to self-reflect.

Maybe the more useful question is how *you* intend to change. If hoped-for improvements in the relationship don't materialize, despite all your efforts, how do you plan to respond? Will you stay entangled in hurt feelings, rage, or withdrawal? Will you get discouraged and feel helpless, getting further ensnarled in the EIP's relationship system and emotional coercion? Or, are you willing to change your approach to the EIP so that you feel stronger and more self-confident, even if they never change?

Whether the EI person changes or not, the roles in the relationship become more equal as soon as you stop granting them the right to tell you how to feel and think. Let's look at how you might begin to do these things.

Strategy

When you can be more objective about an EIP's behavior and your reactions to it, you have a chance to transform the interaction into a more maturely differentiated encounter. Instead of falling under the EI's influence, you can make a point of staying aware of your own values and individuality. To do this, you step back and observe what's happening in every interaction. Instead of going along with their position, you state your thoughts and preferences, communicating with them in an objective, neutral way. You let them know how you will respond to certain behaviors. You stay in an individualized consciousness no matter how they try to pull you into their mindset. The change comes when you can be a separate individual who cares but also doesn't allow them to control you.

Reflection and Discovery

Think of a time when an EIP did something that gave you hope for the relationship's improvement? What exactly did they do that gave you hope?

_____

_____

_____

_____

Have you ever given up hope that this person would change? Recall that moment and describe what it was like to experience that realization.

_____

_____

_____

_____

Tip: What if you learned how to be with EIPs in a way that made you feel in control of yourself and no longer vulnerable to their behavior and reactions? What if you were so comfortable in handling them that it no longer mattered to you if they changed? You would have single-handedly created a better relationship even if they didn't change at all. You always have the power to see others realistically and to experience your own individuality, so you always have it within you to make a relationship with an EIP feel more to your liking.

In the next part of the book, we'll look at how EIPs have affected you and how you can disentangle yourself from the effects of their psychological dynamics.

Part II

How EIPs Have
Affected You

My siblings had the same parents. Why are we so different?

Sibling differences and two types of ACEIPs

Sibling differences are a source of wonder. How can two people with the same parents, growing up in the same home, turn out so differently? Many ACEIPs whom I work with are responsible, self-reflective types—people who seek out therapy and coaching to improve their lives. But many of these people have siblings whose lives are characterized by trouble getting along with people, substance abuse, mental health issues, or enmeshment with parents.

Though ACEIPs fall on a continuum of behavior, there seem to be two distinct types. Let's look at distinct examples of each.

Internalizers

- Tend to be self-aware, self-reflective, perceptive, and sensitive

- Like to reflect on things and love learning

- Try to figure out how to respond advantageously instead of being reactive

- Seem more mature and insightful and tend to be competent and reliable

- Thoroughly process their experiences (Aron 1996)

- Feel a responsibility toward other people

- Are likely to have been "parentified" children (Minuchin et al. 1967; Boszormenyi-Nagy 1984), meaning their EI parents leaned on their capabilities, and relied on them as confidants or helpers

Internalizer ACEIPs tend to like self-help books since they are psychologically curious and enjoy learning about human behavior. They're the ones most likely to seek help for dealing with EIPs because they instinctively cope by gaining insight. Unless otherwise specified, when talking about ACEIPs in this book I'll be referring to internalizers.

Externalizers

- Tend to be excitable and react impulsively, even if they seem quiet or introverted

- Have a low tolerance for stress and take action—even if ill-considered—to blow off tension

- Get themselves in trouble by not thinking about future consequences; they live for the present moment and aren't strategic in how they think about their lives

- Are not self-reflective and externalize blame for their troubles onto other people

- Are angry that so many frustrating and distressing things happen to them but rarely think to question their own behavior as part of the problem

- Can gravitate toward substance abuse or highly dependent or conflictual relationships

- Are likely to be emotionally immature and fall within the EI category

Since there is a continuum linking internalizing and externalizing extremes, many people can show some characteristics of both, or can move toward the opposite end of the continuum under special conditions. For instance, all of us, internalizer or not, tend to become more externalizing and dependent when we're sick, fatigued, or highly stressed. Our tolerance for frustration goes down at these times, and even internalizers may become critical or have a short fuse.

Conversely, externalizers might become more internalizing after they hit rock bottom and their old ways start costing them too much. At this point, they may become more open to guidance and help, especially if they're given support and regular access to helpers upon whom they can depend. Externalizers who examine their lives with self-reflection and accountability can begin to change. Highly structured 12-step programs are designed to support this maturation and self-accountability process. Also, court- or job-ordered counseling might provide incentives for nurturing better self-control and more mature ways of coping.

Overall, the biggest difference between these two approaches to life is that internalizers self-reflect and think about other people's feelings, whereas externalizers are more prone to take tension-reducing action and see others as causing their problems.

Do you have a sense of where you fall on the continuum between internalizer and externalizer? Consider which characteristics remind you more of yourself.

How do we account for these different types of ACEIP? We don't know whether these differences are physically innate, or if they're responses to environmental factors, like quality of parenting or birth order. But we can consider some possible causes underlying the two types to better understand them.

It could be that internalizers were born more neurologically perceptive and sensitive than their externalizer siblings; the parts of their brain they use more or their innate neurobiology could explain how they tune in to other people's feelings with minimal cues. Internalizers also seem more intellectually curious; they like to think and learn, so anticipating consequences comes more easily to them. They're also insight oriented, intrigued by complexity, and looking for underlying reasons for behavior.

Externalizers also may have physiological reasons why they react more strongly and jump into situations with both feet before looking. Their impulsivity and high levels of life drama could be due to inherent difficulties in being able to soothe themselves. It might be that as children they were so physiologically reactive to stress that the optimal development of their thinking function was overwhelmed.

For instance, neuroscientist Stephen Porges (2011) has done research on the differences in neurological and emotional reactivity due to the tone and functioning of a person's ventral vagal nerve. This branch of the parasympathetic nervous system is thought to govern our ability to self-soothe and to recover from fear and emotional distress by seeking comfort from others. Porges thinks that people with high emotional reactivity—like borderline personality disorder, for instance—may start out life with limited neurological ability to rebalance themselves after a threat or an upset. It's as if their bodies are primed to go into an alarm state and stay there, and then they require help to calm down and renormalize.

Whatever the causes, compared to a more self-sufficient internalizer child, a highly reactive child may bring out different behavior in a parent. Difficulties with calming down may lead parents to use immediate gratifications to soothe these children, teaching them that they can't restabilize unless they get special treatment. They thereby miss opportunities to learn how to calm themselves in the absence of immediate gratification.

Parents who overidentify and emotionally fuse with a child also may foster externalizer behavior by treating the child as a proxy for the special attention and gratifications they feel they never got. Such a child might become the parental favorite, causing jealousy among siblings. But this child's position is not enviable, for they stay entangled with a parent who rewards the child for remaining overly dependent. Such a parent is living, in effect, through the child and not allowing them to develop their own individuality.

In contrast, the internalizer child is less likely to elicit enmeshment from a parent because—perhaps due to their heightened perceptiveness and self-awareness—they tend to maintain their own individuality and autonomy even when the parent might like them to be more dependent.

These differences between internalizer and externalizer siblings can lead to hard feelings on both sides. The internalizer feels they are on their own; the externalizer feels like others can never do enough for them. The internalizer might feel burdened with adultlike responsibilities and high expectations, while their externalizer sibling seemingly gets away with everything. Meanwhile the externalizer might resent the responsible internalizer for being a straight arrow who has more success and is always doing the right thing.

Families also form subconscious scripts for their members (Steiner 1974; Byng-Hall 1985); these can be established early in a child's life and contribute to sibling differences as well. Overall, there is probably an interface between a child's physical and psychological vulnerabilities and strengths and what the family needs to feel stable as a unit. Different scripts can result in very different people.

Determining whether you're more of an internalizer or externalizer can help you have more fulfilling relationships, because once you understand your patterns better you can start to change them.

Strategy

Use the questions below to clarify the type of ACEIP with which you identify more. If you're more of an internalizer, it will take conscious effort not to let your empathy take you into self-sacrificing behavior with EIPs. Remind yourself that you are not responsible for fixing other people's mistakes, nor do you have to be so sensitive to others that you lose your own boundaries.

If you're an externalizer, developing your self-reflection ability will empower you to make changes that could lead to happier relationships and more control over your life. Practice being more sensitive to how other people feel, and seek out opportunities to learn self-soothing and stress-management techniques.

Reflection and Discovery

Do you identify more with the internalizer or externalizer characteristics? Which characteristics most reflect who you are?

_____

_____

_____

_____

_____

_____

If you have siblings, how would you describe them in terms of internalizer and externalizer traits?

_____

_____

_____

_____

_____

_____

Tip: If you're an internalizer, be careful not to get sucked into drama triangles (Karpman 1968), in which you play the role of rescuer while seeing others as either victims or villains. Think twice about jumping in to "save" someone before considering the cost to yourself. This is especially important for internalizers who have slipped over the line into codependency (Beatty 1986), in which you take responsibility for the impossible task of transforming other people's lives. Watch any tendencies to overcare or overperform for people who aren't contributing their fair share to your relationship.

12

It's like I don't exist around them. Why won't they listen or take my feelings into account?

Claim your boundaries, subjectivity, and individuality

Thomas's mother, Anna, was very self-centered and opinionated, refusing to respect Thomas's boundaries when making plans to visit him and his family. At one point, Anna's intrusive and overbearing manner exhausted Thomas's patience, and he asked her not to contact him until he let her know he was ready to communicate. Anna then started an email campaign badgering him to change his mind, explaining that she couldn't stop contacting him because her "mother's love" wouldn't let her, repeatedly asking when they could talk, and proposing a schedule for phone calls. It was as if Thomas had never told her what he wanted. In his words, "She doesn't listen to anything I say; it feels like I don't exist in this relationship. No matter what I say, she does exactly what she wants."

Thomas's request for no contact was a statement of his personal need, but it was also a declaration of his individuation from Anna. He was asserting his right to be different from her and to set a boundary. But Anna wouldn't grant him that dignity. In fact, she pushed hard against his right to be his own person who controls his own boundaries. When Thomas spoke up on his own behalf, he was treated as if he hadn't spoken at all.

EIPs seem threatened when others assert their individuality. This is especially true of narcissistic EIPs, since they center everything around themselves and their wishes. They see their desires as morally justified (Shaw 2014), entitling them to demand whatever they want. It's as if other people don't have needs to consider. They often dismiss, "forget," or deny the other person's wishes because differences don't make sense to them. Why would someone want something different from them?

Since EIPs lack sensitivity to your subjective experience, you won't feel seen, heard, or acknowledged. Without such basic respect, you get that feeling that you don't exist for the other person except as a pawn to control. Some EI parents can't even see their children as deserving of common courtesy. As the mother of one of my clients said to her, "You're my child. I don't have to be nice to you."

With such an attitude, there can be no kindness. Real kindness is embedded in empathy (Epstein 2022), something that EIPs often lack. Kindness says *I recognize your existence*. It seems like such a simple thing, but kindness is a complex and mature emotional act made of equal parts recognition, empathy, and emotional sensitivity to a person's whole, unique being-ness. You can't show real kindness or tenderness toward people if you haven't matured to the point where you experience them as sentient individuals separate from yourself.

When you speak up and set a limit, it seems unbelievable that someone would dismiss your request. Being disregarded is exasperating because you feel invisible and discounted, as if you're not allowed a voice in the relationship. EIPs deny, dismiss, or distort any facts they don't like, including your boundaries. As hard as it is to believe, your no is not the final word for EIPs; for them, it's the opening bid for their bargaining.

As EIPs impose their will on you, they refuse to grant you dignity and authority. This makes sense if you realize that they see you as an extension of themselves that they have the right to direct. They don't respect your wishes because to them it's absurd to think that your subjective experiences could differ from theirs. It's as though your right to be yourself doesn't exist unless they grant it first.

Yet the truth is that you *are* in charge of yourself. EIPs may act as though your feelings and preferences don't matter, but that's reality distortion on their part. Once you see that they're attempting to override you or make their wishes more justifiable than yours, you can reaffirm your position. You can't make them be empathic, but it's critically important that *you* take your feelings into account. You don't have to agree to act like you don't exist around them. Unless you grant them the right to run your life, you cannot be controlled by them.

What follows are suggestions for how to respond to anyone—EI or not—who tries to impose their will on you.

Strategy

Boundaries are easier to set when you vividly imagine how it will feel if you allow unaccept-able behavior to continue. Focusing on this unpleasant future keeps you on track whenever you're tempted to give in to an EIP's demands. A neutral tone, repetition, and stonewalling make it harder for them to bulldoze your position. They usually don't listen the first time you set a limit, but as you persist, you become stronger. Repeating your limits gives you great prac-tice with holding your own with EIPs. You can't force them to recognize you or your rights, but you can repeatedly defend your right to your own subjectivity.

However, if you have any concern that an EIP may become aggressive when you set a boundary, please be sure to seek professional or law enforcement help to navigate safe limit setting.

Reflection and Discovery

Think about a time when you needed space or set a boundary with an EIP who didn't respect your wishes or limits. Describe how that felt. Where did you feel that physical reaction in your body? (In future interactions with EIPs, use that feeling as a warning signal to stand up for your boundaries.)

_____

_____

_____

_____

Think about a time when a considerate person respected your boundaries, and describe how that felt. Notice the difference?

_____

_____

_____

_____

Tip: Don't give EIPs power over your psychological comfort. If you crave acknowledgement and consideration from EIPs, you'll further entangle yourself with them. It's much more effective to acknowledge your preferences and respect yourself by sticking to your own boundaries. When you solicit their buy-in, you become part of their emotional system. But when you differentiate yourself and neutrally state what you intend to do, you become emotionally independent.

13

I had to be the responsible one, the little grown-up, my parent's confidant.

Growing up too fast—the high cost of your precocity

Emma was a smart girl who seemed like an old soul—more mature and serious than her peers. She was not impulsive or silly like the other kids, rather she was always thinking one step ahead, like a little adult. Emma had an anxious mother who lacked confidence, and an academic father who related to Emma mostly around intellectual subjects. For Emma, the parent-child relationship felt reversed, with Emma supporting and adjusting to her parents' needs. At times her mother was so unsure of herself that Emma felt she needed to step in and take charge, especially with her younger siblings. Emma's mother used to tell people with pride that Emma had raised her little brothers, not realizing she was revealing that Emma had been overly burdened with responsibility at an early age.

Emma was also her mother's confidant as she complained about her loveless marriage. Emma felt it was her job to keep her mother from getting depressed. With her emotionally remote father, Emma felt more like his audience, asking intellectual questions and being his attentive listener.

Emma didn't know it at the time, but she was trying to be whatever the adults needed her to be to hold the family together. As soon as Emma could, she went to work and paid for her own car and much of her college. She viewed herself as strong and independent, but underneath this confidence she had a sinking feeling that maybe she wasn't as capable as she seemed.

Emma had channeled her intelligence into growing up too fast. From an early age, she had learned that relying on adults led to disappointment, and that it was usually better to take care of things herself. She monitored her GPA and doctor's appointments, and she stayed current on all her school assignments by herself. She functioned as a surrogate mother to her siblings, but neither of her parents was emotionally attuned or interested enough to see that Emma had developmental needs of her own.

Emma never felt that her parents were robust enough for her to push limits with them. It never felt safe to complain, get angry, or challenge her parents' authority; everyone was barely hanging on as it was. She provided her own emotional security by trying to imagine and prepare for every eventuality. Emma looked so serious because she was always thinking and planning about what could go wrong and what she would do if it did. Her intelligence allowed her to turn to her own mind as her primary source of security, mining her natural precocity to meet her own emotional needs (Winnicott 1958; Corrigan and Gordon 1995). With such self-preoccupied parents, Emma depended on her own mind to comfort herself, solve her own problems, and monitor her safety.

If you were a child like Emma, you may remember soothing yourself alone, mentally coaching yourself through difficult situations, and otherwise *using your own thoughts as a stand-in for parents*. Your own mind became a kind of transitional object (Winnicott 2002), like a teddy bear, a comforting thing that provides security in the absence of parental involvement.

But this solution has limits. When you've grown up too fast, you may be shocked in adulthood by how overwhelmed you feel in the face of unforeseen problems. You try to be ready for anything, but an unexpected crisis can trigger childish desperation over having absolutely no idea what to do. This is because there is still a secret child-part of yourself that's susceptible to being overwhelmed, even though on the surface you handle things well. Under stress you may relive deep insecurity from childhood, when you were alone and no one offered to help, back in those early days before your intellect was developed enough to take over.

This anxiety is not a failing; think of it as a PTSD (post-traumatic stress disorder) flashback from taking on more than you could handle at an early age. When you understand where these moments of extreme insecurity come from, they are much easier to deal with. Anybody would feel vulnerable if left unprotected and expected to function beyond their developmental level.

If any of this experience sounds like yours, your successful reliance on your mental ability may have convinced you that all life's problems can be solved intellectually. When you jump into maturity too early, it can be a challenge later to get back in touch with your feelings. In therapy, you may show excellent insight and self-awareness but actually be quite walled off from deeper emotions and needs. That's why it's so important to find a psychotherapist who is comfortable helping you experience and resolve your emotional issues within the therapeutic relationship. Emotionally focused therapy (Johnson 2019) and accelerated experiential dynamic psychotherapy (Fosha 2000, 2004) are excellent therapies for this.

Allowing yourself to get back in touch with your feelings and to depend on others is the cure for self-care precocity. You don't have to be so determinedly self-reliant. Therapy can help you work with your frightened, overwhelmed inner child-self so that you don't feel so alone.

Let's look at some ways to address this deeper source of insecurity now that you can see how it might've developed. It's important to resolve this because underlying emotional insecurities make you more vulnerable to getting entangled with EIP's control moves.

Strategy

Next time you feel in over your head, reach out to the overwhelmed inner child within you (Whitfield 1987; Schwartz 1995, 2022) who had to grow up too fast. Take that immobilized child under your wing. There's no need to feel embarrassed by how shaken you feel at times under stress. Remind yourself that you feel overwhelmed for a very good reason, given how quickly you had to grow up.

You can now treat yourself differently whenever you feel overwhelmed. Try filling in the following blanks to validate your inner child's feelings, which are the source of your insecurity:

Of course you feel _____ *[for example, panicky, desperate, terrified, ashamed] because* _____ *[for example, you were left on your own, you didn't know what to do, your parents never noticed how scared you were, and so forth].*

When such situations come up now, you can comfort your inner child, saying or writing out your experience several different ways until it feels like you've covered *all* the feelings that make the current situation so scary. As you face the feelings and affirm out loud that your reactions make perfect sense, you travel back in time to let your child-self know there is a caring adult (you) on board now. You as an adult have the rationality and experience to handle this situation, step-by-step, even though your inner child may be petrified.

Also remind your inner child that you don't have to magically know everything at once. As an adult, you know that solving problems requires the incubation of insight and a series of steps, and that nobody has all the answers immediately. But to you as an inexperienced child, it probably looked like grown-ups had instantaneous answers for all problems. Now your inner child thinks that if you're going to be able to take care of yourself, you must be like those adults who know everything already. With such an unrealistic expectation of yourself, your precocious maturity collapses and you panic.

Reflection and Discovery

Describe an incident growing up when you had to put on a good face and act more mature than you really felt. When you had to face something alone and didn't know what to do, how did you get through it?

_____

_____

_____

_____

_____

_____

_____

Now think of another difficult time in your childhood when you felt all on your own. If you could go back to that time, what do you wish someone had said to you? What would you want them to know about what you were going through?

_____

_____

_____

_____

_____

_____

_____

Tip: This overreliance on thinking and one's own mind in childhood is one of the reasons why it's helpful for ACEIPs to seek out psychotherapy. As you focus on your feelings, your body sensations, your emotional needs, and retrieving emotional memories, you strengthen your sense of individuality and the right to your own subjective experiences. By accepting these primal feelings and sensations of yours, you feel more present, alive, and engaged, and better equipped to withstand EI pressure. Your intellect is a wonderful aid, but asking it to make you emotionally independent from other people is too much.

Take note if a therapist seems overly impressed by your intellect and maturity, because they may miss the fact that some of these strengths may have their roots in desperation, not healthy development. If a therapist tries to reassure you by commenting on how well you're functioning, they've missed the point entirely. The problem is that you *have* always functioned too well…and began doing so too early.

14

I'm successful and have built a good life, but sometimes I feel like a fake.

Completing your unfinished self-concept

Aliyah was a self-invented success. She not only started her own business but had also received several awards for best consultant in her field. She even took time to set up a charitable arm of her business to mentor and sponsor new talent in developing countries. As the oldest of four children, she was used to looking after others. However, when people praised her success, Aliyah couldn't shake a sense of being a fake.

Aliyah suffered from imposter syndrome (Clance 1985), having trouble accepting and internalizing her success. The enthusiastic appreciation from others didn't match her own deeper self-concept.

Aliyah's intellectual self-evaluation was realistic, but her emotional self-concept was not. In spite of being aware of her strengths, in social situations she often felt inadequate and out of place. She secretly harbored a self-image she described as "orphan girl." Aliyah worried about being poorly dressed, was embarrassed to be in groups where she could be compared to other women, and always felt she was about to be exposed as an interloper among professionals. Even though she was attractive, well dressed, and often complimented for her style, she thought other women seemed more put together.

Growing up, Aliyah had received little financial or moral support from her parents. When they did notice her, their feedback was often critical and laced with irritation. Her plan to go away to college seemed pointless and selfish to them. They didn't understand her ambition to leave and thought she should be content to help out at home and marry someone in the neighborhood. They saw Aliyah only as a part of the family and seemed to have no idea who she really was as a person.

Although Aliyah had benefited from supportive teachers and therapists, as a successful adult she still saw herself though her parents' critical eyes. Because they hadn't valued her unique identity, she couldn't accept her accomplishments as genuine.

If, like Aliyah, you grew up with EI parents, there's a good chance that your self-concept may not match the grown-up image you now project. You may be very competent and yet have that imposter feeling. This self-doubt may make you hesitate to seize opportunities or parlay your success to the next level.

With uninvested parents, there's often a mismatch between our inner and outer selves. We learn to play the part but don't feel our outer success deep within. Take a moment to reflect on this in your own life. Were you helped to feel good about your appearance and abilities as you grew up? Or did you feel you had to invent yourself as you went along?

Many EI parents don't recognize their children's qualities as precious assets to be supported and developed. They are so fixated on the dramas in their own lives that their children's emotional needs are overlooked. For some EI parents, praising their children would make as much sense as complimenting the kitchen table. EI parents see things in simplistic dichotomies; they're not looking for the subtleties of their children's personalities or talents. Their judgments of their children rise and fall with the tides of their moods. Since EI parents are so often irritated and overstressed, it's no wonder their children end up feeling bad about themselves for no reason. Many EI parents probably have no idea that the kind of attention (or lack thereof) they give affects their child's lifelong self-concept.

Adequately mature parents think about their children's future, and they want their children to see themselves and their strengths accurately. These parents point out their children's strong points and admire their positive characteristics to help their children build a solid scaffolding of self-esteem. Sufficiently mature parents have the empathy to sense how important such parental approval is.

Emotional maturity also means that these parents are realistic, and that their feedback is accurate and useful, neither overselling nor undervaluing their children's qualities. Such lucky children find that their acceptance at home is consistent with how the world responds to them. They confidently know themselves and what they're capable of. There's no worry about being fake.

As Aliyah explored her self-concept, she came to a different view of herself. Instead of feeling embarrassed for having big goals, she now realizes that her ambitions come from creative energy, not selfishness. She's come to see herself as a loving person in the way she treats her partner and friends, even though her parents act as if she never does enough for them. While she doesn't feel effortlessly fashionable like some of her colleagues, she recognizes that she has her own style that complements her and supports her goals. Instead of feeling inferior because she has to work at her appearance, Aliyah now appreciates her interest in cultivating good impressions. She still sometimes senses her inner "orphan girl," but now she feels compassion for her rather than embarrassment. Aliyah's self-concept has increasingly become more accurate and nuanced as she makes the effort to find the right descriptors for the person she's become. She now feels like her sense of self comes from the inside rather than balancing itself precariously atop a manufactured identity.

Let's see how you can go about developing or refining a self-concept that is accurate and anchored to your true interests and abilities, rather than to those of your EI parents.

Strategy

There is no real self-esteem without self-knowledge. If your parents didn't know and describe you accurately, you may enter adult life with diminished self-esteem and an uncertain self-concept. You may be aware of your talent and abilities, but unless you know yourself deeply, your achievements may not feel like they belong to you.

If your internal self-concept seems to lag behind your actual abilities and gifts, consider getting help to learn more about yourself. You could use therapy or coaching to put together a newly conscious self-concept that fits you well. You'll always be changing and growing, so make your deeper self-concept a dynamic work in progress. Cultivate feedback from trusted friends, coworkers, or supportive family members about the kind of person you are, and write it down in your journal.

Reflection and Discovery

If asked, how would your parents describe you? Do you think they would describe you accurately now, given who you've become? Or do you think they would still see you as they did when you were a child?

Let's consider the evolution of your self-concept. What was your self-concept in childhood compared to now? How would you describe how family members saw you and how you saw yourself? What about now?

_____

_____

_____

_____

_____

_____

Are you developing new attributes in your self-concept? What do you want to cultivate in your self-concept for future growth?

_____

_____

_____

_____

_____

Tip: Your self-concept is as much an accomplishment as any other developed characteristic. You are constantly constructing yourself as you discover more about who you really are. You don't have to depend on outmoded family roles or birth orders to define yourself; your self-concept can be so much deeper than that. Start with a handful of deep traits about yourself, those things that never change, and then start adding on the little preferences and capabilities that make up your uniqueness. This honest self-description will give you a healthy and secure self-concept, which will offset any imposter worries. Your self-concept should never be less than your actual accomplishments—regardless of what the EIPs in the world think or how they treat you.

Why can't they give me a little positive feedback?

Why EIPs don't recognize your efforts

Sharing positive feelings is one of those intimate, reciprocal aspects of relationships that EIPs have trouble with. They shy away from the emotional intimacy that praise creates between two people. They have no idea how to start or sustain a positive spiral of supportive feedback. Instead, you remain at square one, always trying to earn it with them.

Instead of imagining what their support means to you—and giving it accordingly—many EIPs lack the empathy to build your confidence or make you want to keep trying. Instead, their lack of encouragement is more likely to create confusion or frustration. Tension and unsafety increase in an atmosphere in which you're being evaluated without reassuring feedback (Porges 2017). In the short term, this emotional withholding might make you try harder, but it soon becomes demoralizing because nothing is ever enough.

Mutual joy over a job well done is one of the great rewards of life. We love it when others recognize and celebrate our efforts. It's part of lifting each other up and achieving great things. Empathy isn't just for sad or hard times. We want others to share our feelings when we're happy as well.

EI parents sometimes shame their children for feeling proud of themselves, calling it "egotistical" or "unseemly," but really, who doesn't want to be recognized for their successes, especially by their parents? When parents join in their children's pride of accomplishment, it gives parent and child a special opportunity to appreciate each other. Far from making the child conceited, it makes the child see that accomplishment brings people closer together in very happy ways.

Research has shown that couples who respond reliably to each other's little bids for positive connections have the healthiest relationships (Gottman and Silver 1999). Couples that showed interest in each other's comments, keeping the ratio of positive to negative interactions high, stayed together longer. They had empathy for their partner's attempts to connect and affirmed the gestures. It's easy to see how this would increase the energy, security, and optimism of both partners.

However, EIPs often overlook these bids for recognition, affection, or connection. They're so focused on their own preoccupations that they disregard these little outreaches. They process the other person's comments egocentrically and literally, responding only if they feel it's warranted or interesting. If they're in a bad mood, they might even react with a snide or critical remark. Warmth or validation depends on their mood, not on what you need.

Many EIPs withhold praise as if it were an endangered commodity, as if doing a good job should be its own reward and that appreciation isn't warranted for doing the basics. They don't see why doing what you're supposed to deserves any special treatment. This stingy approach sets up a conditional atmosphere in which people feel judged and stressed, because their best efforts barely reach a baseline. Perhaps the EIP thinks they're setting the bar high to produce excellence, but the people on the receiving end likely feel overextended and demoralized. Life is hard enough without struggling to receive recognition from people who won't give it.

EIPs often act resentful of being expected to give a positive response. But being in any human relationship carries its implicit promises, whether you agree with them or not. It is reasonable to expect that if you're frequently interacting with someone, you two will respond to each other with tact and empathy. That's not needy; that's reciprocity. Managers and teachers who make others feel appreciated are far more likely to get cooperation and high performance from their people. Performance is more likely to improve in an atmosphere of hopefulness than in one of undue stress.

There may be other reasons why EIPs are emotionally withholding. Perhaps they themselves rarely received praise as children or witnessed people encouraging each other. They may be deeply resentful or depressed. Emotionally stingy EIPs don't see the point in giving recognition just because it makes people feel good. It doesn't occur to them that emotional generosity could make life better for everybody. They demand to be impressed before giving any positive feedback. Some highly motivated people may push themselves to excel under these conditions, but many others just get discouraged.

Now, let's look at what you could do to get more satisfying positive feedback from EIPs in your life.

Strategy

Start with the premise that not everybody is aware of your need for positive feedback: they're not depriving you of it; they just don't realize it's important to you. Instead of expecting EIPs to become kinder and nicer on their own, bring their attention to something you've done that you are pleased with. You can be polite and straightforward and ask for recognition. If this doesn't improve things, ask to have a conversation to discuss the kind of feedback you would like to get and why. Explain why the interaction is important to you, and that even a moment of recognition makes life much more satisfying. Some people need it spelled out, so practice asking for exactly what you want. For example, you could explain to them that the praise doesn't have to be effusive but could be just a brief bit of feedback to show that they're noticing your effort.

Reflection and Discovery

Think of an important EIP in your life who rarely praised you. How did it typically go if you tried to get a positive reaction from them? How did their usual reaction make you feel?

_____

_____

_____

In your life now, when a person doesn't give praise or recognition when you've worked hard for it, how do you typically respond? What do you typically do as a result? Does this get you what you want?

_____

_____

_____

TIP: Some EIPs have a way of making you feel naïve or needy if you express an emotional need for recognition. They often justify their emotional withholding with the excuse that grown-ups shouldn't need such extra attention. But they are wrong. We all need it. Our need for praise and appreciation is not infantile; it is the normal reciprocity of social life. The real problem is not your desire for positive feedback; the real problem is their need to keep distance from other people's emotional needs. Wanting to be recognized and treated well by the people around you is a mark of self-respect, not neediness. You shouldn't be made to feel otherwise.

I easily feel guilty, selfish, afraid, and full of self-doubt.

Seeing through emotional coercion

Even though Rayna was a thirty-year-old with her own family, her mother, Julia, dominated her and insisted on frequent visits. By the time she came to see me, Rayna had begun to believe that she had a right to her own life, and that her mother's expectations and control were excessive.

Rayna started setting boundaries and stopped giving her mother so much information about her life. She cut down on her phone calls to her mother, from daily to twice weekly. Julia was furious and accused Rayna of leaving her all alone, even though Julia had a church community and some good friends. Whenever Rayna tried to defend herself, Julia would snap at her with another accusation. As Rayna put it, "I'm better able to reason with my three-year-old than my mother."

Rayna was determined to separate from her mother, but it was hard. "I feel so guilty," she said. "I know I'm doing the right thing to get my own life back, but I wonder if it's worth it. I feel so selfish when she talks like this. What do I do about the guilt I feel?"

Emotionally coercive people use your needs for connection and security against you to make you conform to what they want. Their *emotional coercion* exploits both love and fear. Anyone who cares about someone is susceptible to it, and nowhere is that truer than in the parent-child relationship. Rayna wanted a relationship with her mother, but she didn't want to be forced into more contact than she felt like giving. When she began to set limits, her mother made her feel guilty, ashamed, afraid, and full of self-doubt. Rayna feared that she was being selfish and would regret her choices later if something happened to her mother.

People sometimes claim that no one *makes* you feel anything. This is an empowering thought on the surface, but it doesn't hold up in real life. When someone tries to make you feel bad, even if you reject what they're saying, their body language, facial expression, and voice tone affect you. Nonverbal communication is more powerful than words, and most neurologically normal people will feel the emotional pressure, whether or not they believe what is said.

Like many EI parents, Rayna's mother resorted to emotional coercion when she realized that Rayna was individuating from her. Julia tried to make Rayna feel morally obligated through guilt and shame. Rayna probably was catching the blame for abandonments and betrayals that had happened to Julia long ago. But Rayna had no part in those and shouldn't have been made to feel bad about herself for wanting a life of her own.

When some EIPs get panicky about losing you, they may escalate from guilt to outright intimidation to keep you under their control. For instance, Julia sometimes cried that she didn't care if she lived or died, scaring Rayna into checking on her whether she wanted to or not. Other EIPs wield fear of bodily harm, fear of losing custody of kids, fear of losing one's job, or other threats to one's security—or even one's life. Whatever the fear, it pulls you back under the EIP's control. You might give up your rights to independence just to keep the person from acting against you.

Talk of suicide is an especially effective coercion that strikes fear in most of us. Such threats are extremely hard to handle. Even therapists have a hard time dealing with these situations. But ultimately, one day you may decide that you're not willing to be held hostage by such threats, whether implied or overt. You might get so sick of emotional coercion and the burden of guilt that you want nothing more to do with the person. If you do need to protect yourself emotionally by staying away from the relationship, you can respond at a distance to a threat of suicide, such as by asking the police or community mental health professionals to perform a wellness check on the person.

After being controlled for a long time, you might feel entitled to lose your temper or strike back because doing so feels momentarily empowering. But this will entangle you further in a destructive dynamic. Fighting with EIPs, blowing up at them, or humiliating them could prompt aggression in some, so try to curb such reactions if an EIP seems unstable. Because the stakes are so high, it's important to take their threats of aggression seriously and to keep yourself safe. Expressing your anger directly to an EIP isn't necessary for your freedom. You can enforce your boundaries with calm and neutrality. Over time, you can find other ways of extricating yourself. Freedom starts inside you, not in the middle of a fight.

Now let's look at how to establish individuation when EIPs are pressuring you to conform.

Strategy

If you're willing to maintain contact with the EIP in question, you might be able to negotiate a new normal in your relationship in which you set the boundaries that are a condition for continued contact. You will need to frequently restate your boundaries and to push away the guilt, shame, fear, and self-doubt that arise in the process of getting free of that person's emotional coercion. This is to be expected. Be prepared for these feelings. They are what have kept you prisoner thus far; they won't go away without your conscious insight and refusal to accept them.

Even if your limits make the EIP feel desperate, your job is to stay calm and self-possessed, stating your position over and over, and encouraging them to get more support or mental health treatment in their life instead of expecting you to do it all. You are not the only person who can help them, even if it feels that way in the middle of the emotional coercion. You can explain that you may have to stop contact for a while if they're unwilling to change. You might tell them that you can be in a relationship with them only if they get appropriate help from other people and don't expect you to meet all their needs. This is a reasonable request, even if they distort it as abandonment. They will ultimately have to accept it if you don't back down.

Reflection and Discovery

Think about a time when you set a limit with an EIP in your life and then felt guilty. What made you feel you had done something wrong? Was your bad feeling mostly coming from your conscience or the other person's reaction?

_____

_____

_____

Think about different times you've been emotionally coerced. Is there one EI maneuver that always seems to make you feel guilty, ashamed, fearful, or self-doubting? (If so, being able to spot the coercion can make you immune to this ploy in the future.)

_____

_____

_____

_____

Tip: As soon as you feel guilt, shame, fear, or self-doubt after an encounter with an EIP, sit down, turn your full attention to each feeling, and write about them. Focus on the intensity of the feeling and all the thoughts that accompany it until you get to the bottom of why you're feeling the way you do (Gendlin 1978; Fosha 2000). By staying with the uncomfortable emotions until you fully explore them, you'll realize that they're conditioned childhood reactions that no longer need control you. But if you suppress the feelings, they will continue to rule you in secret, all the more powerful for being ignored.

Remember, EIPs gain power when you don't realize what is going on. That's true for your own unexamined feelings too. Give your feelings room to reach your consciousness and accept the emotional truth they show you. Emotional coercion only works when we fear our feelings and the people who incite them.

17 They always seem morally superior and "righteous."

Narcissistic EIPs and false moral obligation

Narcissistic people are an EI subtype who undermine your sense of yourself as a worthwhile person. Narcissists have the unique ability to make you feel less than—an erasure of your significance as a human being—while making themselves seem special and entitled. Feeling low about yourself around someone is emblematic of the experience of interacting with a narcissistic person. In any interaction, narcissistic people either elevate themselves or diminish you, or both. Whether they raise their self-esteem or lower yours, the net result is the same: the narcissistic person calls the shots by inventing a relationship hierarchy in which they dominate.

Like other EIPs, narcissists lack empathy, but their degree of egocentrism is a cut above other EI types. Narcissistic grandiosity inflates their sense of deservingness far above that of ordinary EIPs. Seeing themselves as superior and entitled, their relationship style is one of jostling for position and domination. To keep them feeling good about themselves, your role is to let them impose their will on you.

Lack of empathy is one thing, but narcissists go one step further. Narcissistic personalities have zero interest in your subjective inner experience (Shaw 2014). They proceed as though you don't have an inner world with your own thoughts and feelings. They refuse to grant other people the same entitlement to existence that they enjoy. Instead, they relegate you to a need-satisfying function in their lives, never thinking to acknowledge your individuality or even personhood.

Narcissistic EIPs claim final say on everything in the relationship because it never occurs to them that you also have rights. Their grandiose sense of entitlement unfurls itself as soon as you show any resistance. They are outraged if you balk at their demands, not only because you're frustrating them, but because you're questioning their fundamental, sacrosanct rule of engagement: people should defer to their opinions and rubber-stamp their wishes.

Narcissistic personalities wield disdain and shame to make you feel irrationally guilty for not going along with their wishes. Their egocentric moral outrage suggests that you have a *moral* obligation to do what they want, and it is so compellingly conveyed that many people fall for it. Narcissists see themselves as deserving and morally righteous in any request because they are certain they are right. When you sense a moral obligation being imposed on you, consider it a red flag telling you to evaluate a person for narcissism.

If narcissistic EIPs only expressed anger when disappointed, it would be easy to see how self-interested they are. But because they act morally superior and condemn your choices as selfish or ill-informed—while questioning your loyalty and moral goodness—you're likely to feel self-doubt. You may even feel the urge to apologize for having differing values and viewpoints. (Narcissistic cult-leaders exploit this fear of being judged to solidify their absolute control.)

Narcissistic EIPs excel at making others feel guilty about setting limits with them. Their temper, coupled with the sting of moral condemnation, makes you feel small. Instead of expressing their feelings ("I'm disappointed and hurt."), narcissistic EIPs deliver moral judgments ("If you were a loving person, you wouldn't be so selfish. You are a bad person who doesn't care about others."). If they shared feelings, you could talk issues through and perhaps find a solution. But their judgment of you as being a villain is a slammed door. Children of narcissistic EI parents can internalize this moralizing voice and feel bad for simply having their own preferences.

Here are some strategies for dealing with narcissistic EIPs.

Strategy

Stop and think the next time someone tries to maneuver you into doing something you don't want to do, especially if you tend to feel guilty when someone acts offended. (Keep in mind that acting like they've been wronged is a very EI thing to do.) *Clarify for yourself whether you've actually done something hurtful or merely offended their sense of exaggerated entitlement.* Many EIPs with narcissistic tendencies are adept at structuring situations so that your options seem limited to the response they want. But you don't have to feel guilty or fall for this forced-choice dilemma. Their preferences don't impose a moral duty. They just don't.

Clarify exactly what they're asking of you. Tell them you need to think it over and will get back to them. Give yourself time and space to decide if you can or want to help, and to determine what you can comfortably manage. Not only will you be taking care of yourself, you'll be protecting the relationship from becoming too one-sided or strained by unfair demands. When you get back to them, offer to help in a way that makes sense to you and don't give more than feels fair. If you can't or don't want to help, offer to think of other options with them, but stay neutral if they try to make you feel guilty. Saddling you with moral obligation is predictable; spot it quickly and refuse to buy into it.

Reflection and Discovery

Remember a time when someone made you feel like a bad person for not doing what they wanted. Describe how they did that and how it affected you.

_____

_____

_____

_____

_____

Pretend someone has implied that you have a moral obligation to do something you don't want to do. Imagine you spot the red flag, observe the reactive guilt or shame that comes up, then imagine yourself stepping back and telling them you'll have to think it over. How do you think you'd feel doing this? How would you like to feel?

_____

_____

_____

_____

_____

Tip: Sometimes the best response to an upset EIP who's mad at you because they can't control you is to not take them seriously. If a child pouted and called you the meanest person ever, you'd understand that their reality is totally dictated by their feelings in the moment. Try the same approach with narcissistic EIPs. Hold your high ground, stay objective, and continue to have whatever level of relationship you prefer. Grant them all the room they need away from you to feel their anger and blame. If you don't take their moral judgments to heart, you can go forward with what feels right to you now. You are not bad, and they are not your judge.

My parent's religion made me feel afraid and unworthy.

Finding your own religion and spirituality

Dave's father was the minister for a small evangelical church, so family life revolved around prayer, going to church, and other activities in his family's religious community. His parents promoted God as a baleful judge and quick-to-anger punisher, laying down for Dave a narrow path to goodness based on the tenets of the church. Dissent wasn't allowed. If people objected, they were shunned and exiled from the church.

Later in therapy, as Dave grappled with his parents' emotional immaturity, his religious ideas began to change. He began to see how closely his parents' description of God reflected their own rigidity and narrow-minded judgments. He wondered: Could God be the ultimate ruler of the universe, yet be as reactive and bitter as his parents? It just didn't fit. As he distanced himself from his parents' rigid ideas, he found it hard to believe in a God who seemed less understanding and compassionate than himself.

One of the most painful parts of Dave's individuation from his family was his loss of spiritual certainty and sense of closeness to God. He felt adrift, unable to find the same security he'd experienced at home and in his church. Even though the God of his childhood had seemed judgmental, Dave at least had felt assured of love and protection—as long as he believed. The updated God of his adulthood seemed more abstract and remote, compared to the frightening but comfortingly omnipotent God of his childhood.

People tend to define *religion* through practices, beliefs, and community rules for engagement, whereas *spirituality* is much more about direct personal experience, such as intuitive knowing and awe-inspired emotional states (G. Vaillant 2009). Traditional religions, with their emphasis on beliefs and codes of behavior, have their home in the organizational parts of the brain that emphasize rules and boundaries. Spirituality, on the other hand, seems to originate in the more emotional, intuitive parts of the brain.

Many self-aware and self-reflective people who value individuality may lean more toward personal spiritual experiences than organized religion. They have spiritual feelings, as most people seem to have the brain potential for (Newberg and Waldman 2009), and prefer to explore spirituality for themselves rather than being told what to believe. In contrast, religion-minded EIPs might gravitate more toward highly structured, hierarchical religious groups that offer a sense of security and certainty. Of course, many different people might enjoy their spirituality within an organized religious community, but rigid, authoritarian formats can be especially appealing to EIPs.

Problems with EI parents may have affected your impression of God and your trust in religion. Kids often form their image of God based on their parents, so how you were treated in childhood may influence your adult image of the divine. It can be troubling and confusing if, as a child, God was described to you as resembling an EI parent: loyal yet vengeful, quick to anger but loving as long as you behave. You may surmise that God, like your EI parents, will withdraw support at the first sign of displeasure. As one person told me: "I know better, but I just can't shake the image of God as an old man on a throne, judging the world." Trusting that you're loved by God is difficult if that love is contingent on approval. The same is true of the love of an EI parent.

EI parents' self-preoccupation can make it hard for their children to conceptualize God as interested or caring. If you based your image of God on the template of your parents' emotional immaturity, God may feel like an unsafe leader, a being who gives love but can suddenly turn on you if you deviate from expectations. You may have grown up thinking that God requires constant worship in order to maintain stability and goodwill toward you—a situation that more resembles what narcissistic EI parents demand. Seeing God as this kind of heavenly parent can be confusing and scary, perhaps prompting you to reject religion altogether.

Another popular religious teaching that favors EIP's attitudes is that children must self-sacrifice and think of others first in order to be considered good people. Since children—and adults—find it nearly impossible to be selfless, this teaching makes them feel bad about themselves, especially if normal self-interest is seen as sin. Holding up altruism as an ideal for impressionable children makes them feel like failures at something for which they're not developmentally ready. With such teachings, religion becomes an unreachable goal, not a comforting help.

Dave ultimately realized that his parents had not given him a workable platform for his emerging spirituality. Their religion instilled fear, unworthiness, and tension instead of loving confidence and inner support. However, Dave missed the security, predictability, and comfort of his early religious practices. While growing apart from his parents' sense of God, Dave felt a little disoriented and uncertain as he processed this sense of loss. He felt as if he were making up his own spirituality out of instinct and intuition alone. He was greatly relieved when he found a more open-minded religious community that offered ritual and ceremony for his spiritual feelings without demanding that he agree with all church teachings or face expulsion.

If your childhood version of religion no longer feels meaningful, you may relate to Dave's struggles. Here are some ideas for empowering yourself to find your own spirituality.

Strategy

What if you start with the assumption that you have the right to explore and discover a form of spirituality or religion that makes you feel stronger and better able to cope with life? What if fear and guilt don't have to be part of the package? What if your individuality could be welcomed? Ask yourself what you need from your spiritual beliefs, and clarify what your personal experience of God or Spirit has been.

If religion is not part of your life, perhaps certain spiritual experiences nevertheless have given you a sense of awe or of belonging to something bigger than yourself. Can you let your spirituality evolve along with the rest of your self, supporting a process of discovery rather than reinforcing constraints? You don't have to give up your individuality to believe in God; in fact, you may find that getting to know your true self and claiming your individual rights will add to a more richly dimensioned spirituality.

Reflection and Discovery

What was the emotional tone of the spiritual beliefs you were taught growing up? How were you supposed to feel about yourself vis-à-vis God?

_____

_____

_____

_____

_____

_____

_____

Now, as an adult, what spiritual beliefs are the most compelling for you? How do you see your relationship with God? How do your current beliefs support your ability to cope with life's problems and to love others?

_____

_____

_____

_____

_____

_____

_____

_____

_____

_____

Tip: Ultimately, you have the right to discover your own spirituality. Finding a welcoming spiritual community that values your individuality may allow you to develop your spiritual side in a way that feels supportive and freeing instead of submissive. Finding like-minded people can also join spirituality with emotional connection. In such an environment, spiritual feelings may arise in new ways that enrich rather than limit you. Since spirituality and positive, nurturing emotions (such as love, faith, hope, and awe) are so connected (G. Vaillant 2009), seeking more love, compassion, and community in your life may open you up to a more rewarding and less ambivalent kind of spirituality.

I was taught to believe things about myself that just aren't true.

When self-criticism reflects old brainwashing

Bonnie was a great problem solver at work, but at home she criticized her performance ruthlessly, calling herself out for being "stupid," "careless," or "embarrassing." Sometimes this self-flagellation was so severe that Bonnie felt depressed and dejected for days. Bonnie's self-image was split into two parts: a reasonable, problem-solving adult versus a reviled screwup who couldn't do anything right. When her self-critical part took over, she really believed that making mistakes called for merciless self-abuse.

Like many ACEIPs, Bonnie had learned to shame herself from her parents, who thought the best way to socialize her was to come down hard on her for mistakes. They regularly told her how stupid and careless she was, implying that if she had been more careful her mistakes wouldn't have happened in the first place. Instead of rebelling, Bonnie agreed with their assessment. As an internalizer, she too could always find the places where she went wrong. Resolving to never make a particular mistake again, Bonnie tried extra hard to be perfect and keep on everyone's good side.

In her book on brainwashing, neuroscientist Kathleen Taylor (2004) describes how isolation, control, absence of outside support, helplessness, and the breakdown of one's sense of self and identity add to the effectiveness of brainwashing. Such conditions almost exactly parallel a child's vulnerability with their parents. While most parents would deny brainwashing their children, authoritarian EI parents, such as Bonnie's, unwittingly use similar thought-reform tactics to influence their kids' minds. Bonnie internalized her parents' critical voices and resolved to be perfect. She was like a victim of brainwashing who'd accepted the beliefs of her captors. Let's consider another example.

Whenever Sandra resisted or disagreed with her mother's wishes, her mother told her she was selfish and heartless. Once, when Sandra needed to adjust shopping plans with her mother due to childcare arrangements, Sandra's mother angrily snapped, "Just forget it! It's clear you don't want me to go! You are so selfish. You don't love me and never have!"

Sandra reassured her mother and convinced her to not cancel their outing. Many similar episodes over her lifetime had planted the message that Sandra was selfish and unloving. These criticisms, totally outside of Sandra's control, had infiltrated her psyche. She automatically felt like a bad person whenever her mom got mad.

Both Bonnie and Sandra knew that their mothers were overreacting and emotionally impaired in some ways, but that didn't change the fact that deep down they were internalizing the criticisms. Their mothers' overreaction produced an emotional shock that made Bonnie feel worthless for making mistakes, and Sandra feel uncaring and thoughtless if she had needs of her own. This emotional intensity is also an effective factor in brainwashing (Taylor 2004).

In order to succumb to brainwashing, one needs to internalize a captor's messages, and this internalization happens most easily in a context of high emotional arousal. What could be more emotionally arousing than being a child and having an angry adult in your face? This is one way that parental overreaction can resemble brainwashing.

Children like Bonnie and Sandra learn to engage the reflex of self-attack following any behavior they regret. By beating critics to the punch, there is less suspense and more control. The thinking is that if you criticize yourself first, maybe other people will refrain from doing it. It's not a healthy habit, but for many ACEIPs it's preferable to being caught off guard by an angry attack from an EI parent—or from any EIP.

Thankfully, no ordinary EI parent has the skills or intent of a real brainwasher. As a child, you were not actually a prisoner. Your parents' actions probably weren't methodical enough to qualify as brainwashing, and you may have had access to outside support. Nonetheless, their reactivity may have gotten stuck in your mind in the form of self-criticism that you deal with every day.

Fortunately, you can change many negative or inaccurate self-beliefs as you grow up and get fairer feedback from others. There is also a developmental readiness in late adolescence and early adulthood to try on new ideas and to question what you've been taught. You might find a supportive partner or best friend who sees the good in you. For many ACEIPs, distorted beliefs about their value can change when they leave home and are exposed to wider fields of thinking, such as in college, through travel, or at new jobs.

But even as your world expands, negative self-beliefs can persist or resurface, particularly in interactions with EIPs. Here are some ways to figure out where your beliefs came from, and how to negotiate a change in attitude.

Strategy

First, ditch the idea that feeling terrible about yourself is a sign of a healthy conscience. Feelings that make you feel bad and hopeless about yourself are not linked to facts; they're linked to painful memories and simply aren't true.

The next time an interaction with an EIP leaves you feeling self-critical, write down the beliefs about yourself that are circling in your mind. Get your self-criticisms on paper so you can look at them objectively. Feel empathy for the child in you that was made to believe such discouraging lies. Ask your adult mind to weigh in on these beliefs and present evidence for why they are not true. Reconsider these beliefs once a day for a couple of weeks until you feel the beliefs begin to soften and shift.

Your parents probably came down hard on you because there was something that scared them. Pretend you are your parent back then and try to intuit what that might have been. Imagine yourself as your parent and complete this prompt (Ecker and Hulley 2005–2019):

I criticized you by _____ *because I was afraid that* _____.
(For instance, *I criticized you by giving you disgusted looks because I was afraid that you'd embarrass the family.*)

It doesn't matter if your interpretation is true; the point is to consider that your parents' critical barbs were self-defensive rather than objectively justified.

You can also try writing out a conversation with the part of your personality that criticizes you and brings you down (Schwartz 1995, 2022). Ask it why it thinks it necessary to treat you so meanly to get its point across. Record its response and see if you agree. If you don't, ask it if it'd be willing to try a different approach with you.

You can work with that aggressive, critical part of yourself to pursue gradual self-improvement rather than self-demolition. Ask that part if it would be willing to help you in a more considerate way. See if that part would be willing to transform its role to that of more of a trusted friend or mentor, someone who wants the best for you and offers gentle feedback. How would this more compassionate mentor-voice talk to you? (For more about working with negative personality parts, see Richard Schwartz's book *No Bad Parts*).

Here are some other techniques for dealing with distorted beliefs.

Reflection and Discovery

Pick two distorted beliefs or thoughts you developed as a result of criticisms from EI people. For example:

A belief about yourself as a person

_____

_____

_____

A belief about the world or other people

_____

_____

_____

Write down alternative beliefs that update the two you noted above.

_____

_____

_____

_____

_____

Tip: You believed critical things about yourself because someone said them frequently or delivered them with emotional intensity, or both. These thoughts wormed their way into your deepest worries about yourself. However, using the same tools of repetition and emotional investment, you can update old programming. Angry EI people in the throes of emotional meltdowns shouldn't be allowed to construct the foundation of your self-concept. Their loss of control needn't stay in your mind, nor should their angry voice be what you hear in your head. Turn your energy toward solving problems from this point forward, rather than continuing to tear yourself down with internalized voices from the past.

20

I get overly emotionally involved in the EIP's needs and problems.

Stop emotional takeovers and overidentification

Emotional takeovers happen when EIPs make you care more about how they feel than you do about yourself. It's called a "takeover" because they disregard you as a person and expect you to meet their needs immediately. When an EIP has a problem, they make you feel like you should put your life on hold and give them whatever they want.

EIPs get away with emotional takeovers because they make it seem like their urgent needs should come first, and that nothing in your life is as significant as what they're going through. They send the message that if you were a decent person, you wouldn't hesitate to give them anything they need. Their assumption is that since you have so much, it would cost you nothing to make them happy. In a nutshell, you're coldhearted if you don't help immediately.

If you grew up in an EI atmosphere, chances are that a part of you *does* believe their assumptions. Remember, the central goals of their emotionally immature relationship system are for you 1) to stabilize them emotionally and 2) to shore up their fragile self-esteem. Without your compliance, they threaten to become angry or fall apart under stress. Their distress, like that of an infant, upsets you so much that you'll do whatever it takes to soothe them.

When EIPs feel overwhelmed by a stressful situation, it's an emergency to them. Their emotions magnify and warp their problems into something cataclysmic, creating what psychologist Brian Wald calls a "distortion field" through which everything looks worse than it is. *Emotional contagion* (Hatfield, Rapson, and Le 2009) then pulls you into their fear and helplessness, convincing you that *something must be done immediately!* Their distortion field convinces you that *their* distress is an emergency in *your* life, something you must devote yourself to until you solve it for them. Caught up in the takeover, you emotionally fuse with them (Bowen 1978) and take on the rescue mission.

Emotional fusion with an EI person feels like being on call 24/7. You're expected to do whatever this frantic, emotionally unstable person—in their panic—thinks is necessary. You're expected to hop to it and manufacture a solution out of thin air. You feel stuck in something that you want to be as far away from as possible. Responding with reason, questioning assumptions, considering alternatives, sleeping on it, or researching information are seen as pointless delays to EIPs, who see such responses as uncaring and cold.

Yet these actions may be just what's needed. You don't have to make their urgency your problem. If it feels like they are demanding your help, you have the right to stop right there. Pressure should be your signal to back up and think.

Overidentifying with the EIP's pain or upset is at the heart of an emotional takeover. When you overidentify, you make their suffering your own and feel their distress even more than they do. For instance, overidentification causes you to agonize over what they're going through, how embarrassed they must be, how powerless they are, how excruciatingly grief-stricken they must feel, and so on. Overidentification happens so instinctively that some people believe they're literally picking up the other person's pain like a radio wave. More likely, they're just vividly imagining everything they think the other person might be going through.

For example, a client of mine described sobbing on the floor after a phone call from her mother informing her that her mother's brother had died. She felt like her mother's pain had flowed right into her, even though she herself was not particularly close to her uncle. Another client, a young man, felt hot-faced humiliation when his father awkwardly tripped and fell at a family gathering; he found himself crying later as he thought about how mortified his father must have been. These adults had very permeable boundaries with their parents and felt the only way to be loyal and loving was to feel the parent's pain completely. They were showing their loyalty to emotionally remote parents by overidentifying with their experiences with an excess of empathy.

Whatever the reason, overidentification with others' suffering can be harmful to you. You may think you're showing your love by taking on the other person's pain, but because overidentification is highly exaggerated empathy, you can actually suffer more than the other person. Realistic empathy gets lost in overamplified, imagined pain.

If you've been prone to emotional takeovers, and overidentification, let's put an end to it. You don't have to be so consumed by the experiences of EIPs that you lose yourself. Letting yourself get overly entangled won't help them one bit. Real caring and comforting does not require fusion and self-sacrifice. Let's take a look at ways to prevent these moments of emotional takeover and overidentification.

Strategy

Emotional takeovers start with the implicit agreement between you and the EIP that their feelings are more important than anyone else's. Here are some steps for evading a takeover:

1. First, realize that your feelings and welfare are just as important as theirs. As fellow adults, the needs of *both* people matter.

2. If you start to feel panic or urgency over their problem, observe your reaction, back up, and detach. Try to regain objectivity and calmness. Stay aware that the ultimate responsibility in the situation is theirs.

3. Say a few comforting words if you want, ask for time to think their problem over, and get back with them only after you've reclaimed a sense of entitlement to your own life.

4. Don't get back with them until you're sure your response feels doable and agreeable to you. The secret power of emotional takeovers is that EIPs always present their problems as being so urgent that you can't take time to think. Instead of falling into their chaos, ask for their patience while you consider all sides of their request. By the time you get back to them, they may have moved on to someone else. Emotional takeovers are only satisfying for EIPs when others unquestioningly entangle themselves in their problems.

Overidentification can't get a foothold unless you agree that the EIP's feelings are more important than anything else in the situation. When you start to imagine every gory detail of their distress, catch yourself, and then purposefully dial it back. Remind yourself, *This is not happening to me. I can be caring without making this my pain. Fusing with them is harmful, not healthy.* One client described this process as "finding the boundaries within my own mind."

Overidentification is not proof of love; it's a sign that you're getting absorbed in another person's life to an unhealthy degree. Proportionate empathy is sufficient caring; you needn't try to feel their worst pain.

Reflection and Discovery

Remember a time when you got caught up in an EIP's emotional takeover and overidentified with their problems. Describe in detail what that felt like.

_____

_____

_____

_____

_____

_____

_____

If you had known about emotional takeovers, distortion fields, and overidentification, how might you have responded differently to the EIP?

_____

_____

_____

_____

Tip: Let EIPs have their pain in just the way that's right for them. It's not up to you to take it on. Nobody should be expected to do that for another person. You can love and be loyal without wringing yourself out. Practice giving empathy, but don't make it your responsibility to make up for all the pain they've ever experienced—an impossibility if ever there was one.

21

I can't think straight around them.
I get confused and inarticulate.

Clearing up brain scramble

Karyn felt prepared for her visit home with her folks. She knew they'd disapprove of her plans for a job change, but she had planned out the conversation. She didn't want to keep her job move secret and was ready to practice some boundaries. She felt ready for the barrage of unsolicited advice they'd give her.

But when Karyn returned from her visit, she felt utterly defeated. Her parents had been alarmed by her plans, and her intended limit-setting evaporated. She ended up listening to their concerns and feeling increasingly incapacitated and self-doubting as they wore on. Now she was angry at herself for letting them push her around.

"I feel ashamed of myself for not being more effective with them," Karyn said. "I couldn't hold my focus about what I wanted and needed. I couldn't communicate; I felt I was confusing everyone. They put me in an absolute spin. I couldn't even think. My mind went totally blank. I was almost stuttering."

Karyn's sense of befuddlement had a deep history with her parents: "If you tell me I did something wrong, I assume you're right. I'm trained to think I'm wrong."

Karyn noted that this problem occurred when she tried to communicate with difficult or imperious people. Although she prepared herself in advance to deal with her parents, being face-to-face with them left her flustered and confused. She thought this was a sign of her weakness and felt very discouraged.

You, too, may experience what therapist Jenny Walters calls "brain scramble" when you try to talk about something important to an EIP. Like Karyn, anyone who tries to get their point across to EIPs would likely come away from a similar encounter feeling like a communicative failure. The problem lies not in you, but in the EIPs who aren't interested, listening, or responding.

If you say something an EIP doesn't like, they will reject your reality. It's their favorite, all-purpose defense. It keeps them feeling secure and in control. For her EI parents, Karyn's news about her job change was not a fact for them to accept, but something to deny and dismiss. Because EIPs aren't interested in your inner world or subjective experience, they aren't motivated to try to understand. With their one-track mind (*How will this affect me?*), they're only aware of how the situation makes *them* feel. They may disguise their rejection as concern for you, but basically they're resisting a change they dislike.

EIPs are also uncomfortable with the emotional intimacy aroused when you talk to them about something you truly care about. It's too much closeness. They sense your sincerity and emotion, and they recoil. Instead of hearing you out, they seize upon anything that supports their viewpoint and tune out everything else. You're left confused because you thought you were being straightforward and perfectly clear. Their responses don't make sense because they're responding more to their own anxiety and pet concerns rather than what you said.

When you sincerely try to communicate and an EIP goes off on a tangent, you're stopped in your tracks. You don't know what to do next. Should you restate your message? Figure out what they're saying and why? Try to find a way to link their response to what you said? There's no good answer because their self-involved response didn't follow logically or make sense. They leave you puzzled and unsure of yourself. But that's not weakness; it's EI-induced confusion.

The curveball of EI illogic disrupts your thinking. When you try to follow their point, you get lost in confusion. At that moment of bafflement, you are now ripe for their suggestions and control. Once you're off balance, you become their audience and start following their lead. They're not fiendishly plotting to use mind control on you; it's just that when they get uncomfortable their EI defensiveness instinctively kicks in to derail your message. They automatically disrupt and destabilize any interaction that threatens to take them where they don't want to go.

It's impossible to communicate with a person who doesn't want to listen or understand. It's very hard to keep your train of thought with someone who is clearly unreceptive. If you're an emotionally connected person, you look for eye contact, gestures of agreement, signs of puzzlement, or anything that shows the other person is trying to understand you. When EIPs instead seem distracted, uninterested, or disapproving, it's easy for your motivation to fizzle and for brain fog to roll in. Feeling opposed before you even finish talking makes it hard to remember what you were trying to get across.

Karyn had trouble because she opened the door to her parents' opinion about her decision. She thought that her clarity would stand up to their disapproval, and so she listened to what they had to say. Unfortunately, she lost sight of her right to not engage in *any* discussion with them. Instead of trying to explain herself to them, she might have casually and briefly informed them of her job change while explicitly refusing discussion or feedback. She could have told them her news in a neutral setting, like a restaurant, where she wouldn't feel trapped, informing them she had made up her mind and wouldn't be discussing the topic further today. Then she could have changed the subject, or left if they refused to stop talking about it. In this way, Karyn could have deflected their tangential, confusing remarks and wouldn't have felt like she had to process their reactions seriously. She could have communicated her news without feeling she was then obliged to listen to their commentary.

Let's further clarify how you can avoid brain scramble and those frustrating conversations that go nowhere.

Strategy

Don't try to make sense out of nonsense. You know what you said, and you know if the EIP's answer wasn't on topic. Notice their tactic but don't try to fix it. Recognize that you are being diverted into brain scramble. Don't try to understand why they're doing it; just stick to the one point you want to get across, using short, clear sentences. Don't let yourself be pulled into discussing anything you don't want to.

Rather than having open-ended goals, approach uncomfortable communications with a succinct plan. Be prepared for evasion and emotional coercion. Don't try to win by getting them to see your point, and don't accept discussion or feedback. Say what you need to say in a light and neutral way and don't expect a productive or helpful response. If you limit your communication with an EIP to simple facts, you'll come out feeling less confused or hurt.

Reflection and Discovery

Have you ever experienced brain scramble when talking to an EIP in your life? Describe the incident, how they reacted, and what made you lose track of what you wanted to say.

How might you proceed differently in the future if you had something important to tell an EIP? Now that you know about brain scramble, what will be your plan?

_____

_____

_____

_____

_____

_____

Tip: Trying to persuade or argue with EIPs is where you're most likely to fall into confusion. Be ready for them to corkscrew the conversation away from you and toward their own issues. If you are clear with yourself that you're trying to inform, not sell, you will communicate whatever you need to. Seeking their input or blessing is a bridge too far.

I can't stand up to them.
They always win.

Spotting the Four Horsemen of self-defeat

Aaron, a young attorney, had a difficult mentor in his law firm. He didn't want to complain, but he was doing a lot of extra work as the older man exploited his time. In addition, his mentor was highly critical, to the point that Aaron finally requested a transfer. This fostered ill will with the mentor, and Aaron continued to feel picked on by him. Aaron began feeling depressed and sought treatment.

Aaron's work experiences reminded him of painful childhood memories of emotional loneliness and helplessness, feelings that made him turn inward and feel like giving up. When I asked if he'd reached out for help back then, Aaron said, "I can't actually imagine what it would be like to ask for help. It's like, 'Why bother?' I just collapse and find ways to comfort myself."

It would have been tempting to tell Aaron that he should have asked for help sooner, since his inactivity perpetuated his suffering. But his dilemma, rooted in early EI relationships, was more complicated than that. Aaron was stuck in passivity because early in life his EI parents had taught him the following rules about the futility of expecting compassion or assistance:

- Nobody notices your distress because no one is monitoring your emotional well-being.

- It's your job to handle your emotional pain yourself.

- You'll feel worse if you ask for help because you'll be made to feel ashamed and inadequate for complaining.

- People will think you're a whiner and avoid you if you need too much help.

ACEIPs as a group are vulnerable to being exploited at work and in relationships because they often lack the sense of healthy entitlement that would compel them to speak up for what they need. If you're like this, you may worry that your needs will make you a nuisance to other people. You may have to push yourself to complain or even to ask necessary questions. Simply put, you may fear your requests will bring disdain or ridicule.

As a result, you can get stuck in self-defeating reactions instead of speaking up for yourself. I call these reactions the Four Horsemen of self-defeat: passivity, dissociation, immobilization, and learned helplessness. You may have turned to these internal ways of coping because your more active efforts made you feel—like Aaron—worse instead of better.

Let's look at these coping styles more closely and see if you recognize any of them.

Passivity is the feeling that it's just easier to give in. People who are trained to put others first often develop this coping style. As a child, you are no match for the entitlement of EIPs, so they can easily pressure you into giving in to their demands. Your naturally active, assertive instincts get tamped down, creating internal conflicts that generate anxiety instead of action. Some children do rebel and resist their parents, but sensitive internalizer children like Aaron are more likely to pull back and try to figure things out on their own. Passivity can be a welcome way to avoid conflict with overbearing EIPs.

Dissociation is a more serious defense than passivity because it separates you from yourself. It usually starts in situations too overwhelming to process, but once you get the knack of it, you might use it a lot. Dissociation can create out-of-body or even amnesiac experiences, but usually it takes milder forms, such as zoning out, numbing yourself with food or substances, or feeling empty and not present. Dissociation can also make you feel spaced-out, distant from your surroundings, or like a situation is surreal or virtual. You don't feel your own reactions anymore and become a disconnected observer in your own life.

While dissociation is more of a mental or existential spaced-out coping style, *immobilization* is an involuntary full-body shutdown. It happens when you feel physically "scared stiff" or frozen. This is the deer-in-the-headlights moment, where you're so stunned by shock you're unable to react. People and animals alike experience this ancient autonomic nervous system reaction when confronted with a mortal threat. An upset EIP can be so intimidating that they trigger this response.

Finally, *learned helplessness* (Seligman 1972) is a state of mind that comes from repeated inescapable experiences that teach animals and people that giving up is the only option left. Interestingly, animals and humans don't have to be deliberately trained to become helpless; they will naturally develop helplessness under conditions of unremitting adversity (Maier and Seligman 2016). This means that helplessness can be a natural response to chronic suffering not under our control, such as that at the hands of EIPs. All the more reason to have compassion for yourself and to understand that feelings of helplessness arise involuntarily and are not a personal failing.

Let's look at some things you can do to overcome these tendencies toward self-defeat when interacting with EIPs. Keep in mind that small steps work best as you try to be more active on your own behalf.

Strategy

Going from passive to more active when interacting with EIPs is an ongoing project. Don't feel that you have to stand up to EIPs all at once. They're unlikely to respond constructively to such efforts anyway. Trying to be effective with them is like trying to nail Jell-O to the wall; they won't go along with what you say and will evade your best efforts to get the response you want. Instead of trying to make them pay attention, figure out what you have control over in an interaction and pursue that outcome. For instance, once Aaron realized his mentor was going to keep exploiting him, he could've sought support from another senior partner or gone to the HR department to report a toxic work environment. Aaron had control over seeking outside help, but not over making his mentor care about his feelings.

When you feel yourself beginning to zone out or become immobilized, step away to a private space, do some steady conscious breathing, and tune in to what you're feeling in your body, alternately tensing and relaxing your arms and hands. This body focus will keep you in touch with yourself instead of dissociating. Reconnecting with yourself and staying present in your body helps you to unlearn passive, dissociative habits so you can take care of yourself more assertively when you need to.

You don't have to be an action hero. It's not how forcefully you speak up; it's how many times you're willing to say the same thing. Even actions that look small and meek will still get you where you want to be. Repeat yourself until you're satisfied you've made yourself clear. Know what you're going to do ahead of time and then do it. Just don't expect to change or persuade EIPs in the process. Even action heroes can't do that.

Reflection and Discovery

Who in your life has made you feel especially powerless or helpless? How exactly did they shut you down? Describe the kind of behavior that is most likely to make you passive and hesitant to act.

_____

_____

_____

_____

_____

_____

Which defensive state—passivity, dissociation, immobilization, or learned helplessness—is most familiar or problematic for you? Describe how it—and other forms of self-defeat—has impacted your life at times.

_____

_____

_____

_____

_____

_____

Tip: EIPs can only defeat you if you're unclear with yourself about what you want. Acting on your own behalf doesn't have to be aggressive or awe-inspiring. Just stay authentic and true to yourself when others put on the pressure. Make sure you notice every time you actively stand your ground, and give yourself plenty of praise. It's a good idea to record these moments in your journal because they're easy to forget. When you spend less time with the Four Horsemen of self-defeat, you'll have more time to go after what you want in life.

I am so angry at them; I can't stop thinking about what they've done.

Lingering anger, resentment, and rage

EIPs tend to stir up anger in other people. Sometimes their insensitivity can make you furious to the point that you can't stop thinking about it.

It's easy to understand why EIPs trigger anger; anger is a natural reaction to feeling dismissed, invalidated, overruled, or controlled. When an EIP doesn't want to hear your point of view, tries to direct your life, or disregards your wishes, it can make you mad. This is especially true when they don't respect your boundaries and keep pushing their agenda.

EIPs also can provoke you into taking on *their* unresolved anger. For instance, they might do infuriating things but maintain their innocence and act like you're the one with the problem. In the previous chapter, Aaron's mentor was such a person. He rationalized his bullying as giving Aaron much-needed training; he would've denied having been angry at Aaron. Instead, Aaron was the one who internalized his mentor's disowned anger and felt provoked by the situation. Such EIPs keep pushing your buttons until there's a fight, but they'll be unaware of their own anger. If you don't realize they're projecting their disavowed anger onto you by provoking you, you may blindly join in their hostility and not realize you've "caught" their anger.

When you can't stop feeling angry while interacting with someone, it's worth considering if the other person might have goaded you into carrying and expressing their unresolved anger. This is the process of *projective identification* (Ogden 1982), in which people subconsciously incite other people to take on their own denied feelings and wishes. This is one of the ways that unresolved emotional issues get unconsciously transferred across family generations (Bowen 1978; Wolynn 2016).

Aside from these psychologically complex sources of anger, there are more obvious causes too. Domineering EI parents are especially likely to provoke anger when they refuse to honor your *mental freedom* or *emotional autonomy*. Such people don't just criticize your behavior, they literally tell you what you should think and feel.

EI parents often stir up anger by prohibiting their children's mental freedom, policing their children's thoughts with blame, shame, or moral judgment ("Don't you dare even think that!"). Some EI parents even put their children in a terrible bind with religious prohibitions. For example, telling a child that having hateful or angry thoughts is as bad morally as actually hurting someone. Such policing doesn't help children deal with their feelings, and then on top of that they're supposed to control the thoughts that pop into their head. Being burdened with such impossible expectations can stir up more frustration and anger.

EI parents also interfere with their children's emotional autonomy by forbidding or punishing any show of feelings. These parents do this due to their aversion to strong, authentic emotion (McCullough et al. 2003). Also, EI parents have a low threshold for emotional stress and can get angry at their children for overwhelming them with their distress, sorrow, or even joyful exuberance. In more supportive families, parental interest and empathy steady the child and make them feel safely contained while upset (Winnicott 2002). In contrast, EI parents just make things worse, piling on and punishing the child for expressing feelings. As a result, the child not only feels upset but unsafe, misunderstood, and angry.

Alongside anger may come hatred. This cousin to anger can be a response to being treated without fairness or empathy. However, hatred toward a loved one—even if involuntary—stirs up a primal sense of guilt. Children naively feel guilty for having such bitter feelings because they don't realize that hatred is an expectable response to feeling controlled or coerced.

When anger at someone cannot be safely expressed, it may be turned against the self in the form of self-criticism or even self-harm. Such self-attack gives the anger an outlet while simultaneously hiding the cause of the anger. Internalizer ACEIPs may feel less guilty directing their fury and hatred at the self, instead of confronting the person who has frustrated or intimidated them.

Ruminating on anger tightens bonds rather than loosening them. If you're stuck in anger when it comes to an EIP, you are still very actively entangled with them. Your anger may keep you reacting to this person many times a day, as if you're still fighting their control. Of course, they no longer have control over you as an adult, but your old anger might be hiding the worry that they could take over again. Fortunately, they can only take over if you unwittingly go along with them.

If you still feel anger toward an EIP, you may be holding on to it because a part of you hopes to force the person to have a more emotionally genuine relationship with you. Perhaps some part of you fantasizes that your anger will prompt them to reflect on their part in the difficult relationship. Anger can be a paradoxical way to keep your distance while still feeling engaged with them.

Finally, your anger may be based on the belief that an EIP is more capable of change than they really are. Your anger says they *could* change, if only they weren't so stubborn. But your anger gives them too much credit. It's more likely that the EIP is a defensive, empathically challenged human being with deep-seated issues who may never be able to give you the understanding that you want. With such people, it can be easier to stay angry than to accept that they are profoundly limited in their ability to relate as an emotionally available adult.

Let's look at some ways to address anger you may feel toward EIPs in your life.

Strategy

The next time you feel your anger welling up while thinking about an EIP, imagine that it's coming from a part of yourself that's trying to protect you and wants only the best for you (Jung 1997; Schwartz 2022). Pretend you're interviewing this part of yourself and trying to understand it. You can do this in your head, by talking aloud, or by writing down the dialogue in your journal.

Express curiosity about this angry part of yourself and invite it to talk to you, like another person. By asking it questions, without trying to direct its answers, you'll gain empathy for yourself and maybe see why you've been so angry. Such internal conversations might get you closer to *all* your feelings, not just anger.

By understanding all the different purposes your anger might be serving, you can ask yourself how much longer it might be needed, and whether its strength could be channeled into something that could bring you more satisfaction.

Reflection and Discovery

When you were growing up, what was your family's attitude toward angry or hateful feelings? Did they expect you to suppress them, or did they give you guidance? What did your parents teach you about what to do when you felt angry?

_____

_____

_____

_____

_____

Think of a time when you stayed angry with someone for a long time for something they did to you. How did you wish they had responded to your anger? How did you hope your anger might affect them?

_____

_____

_____

_____

_____

Tip: At some point, plan a reckoning with your anger. Is it serving a purpose, or interfering with your life? Using the ideas above, determine what else might be going on in you alongside the angry feelings. Don't try to get rid of your angry feelings before you've gotten to the bottom of why they're there. If you need to stay angry, consciously enjoy the empowerment it brings until you find more rewarding ways to process what happened to you. As you feel more comfortable with your rights as an individual, you may find your anger no longer feels so necessary.

I've had some disappointing relationships. How do I do it right next time?

Looking for emotional maturity in a partner

Perhaps the biggest relationship stumbling block for any ACEIP is over-tolerance for one-sided relationships. Instead of looking for a kind, responsive partner who sees and emotionally supports them, ACEIPs can be drawn to unfinished beings, people who need reminders to think of others or to be more emotionally intimate. Many ACEIPs may tough out such relationships in the hope that life's developments—such as getting married, having children, buying a house—eventually will lead to more maturity and closer connections. However, additional responsibilities aren't likely to make things better unless the people involved have evolved.

If you grew up around egocentric EIPs, you probably expect to do a lot of emotional work in your relationships. For instance, you may compensate for a partner's emotional immaturity by managing communication, initiating discussions, making amends, and trying to improve the connection. By doing so, you tacitly agree to be the grown-up in the relationship. Unfortunately, this is a setup for codependent relationships (Beatty 1986) in which you take on too much responsibility for another person's recovery or growth, to the point at which you can lose yourself.

Do you interpret disappointing behavior as a warning sign, or as an invitation to rehabilitate a person? Was it your hope to teach empathy to your partner and to coach them toward emotional accountability? Where did you learn that relationships are such hard work?

If you've had an unsatisfying relationship in the past, how do you make the right choice next time? A good start is to notice how a person treats you, especially in stressful situations.

It sounds simple, but if you grew up with EIPs, you've been trained *not* to notice how you're being treated. Difficult people show signs early that they have trouble with empathy, emotional intimacy, impulse control, stress tolerance, and respect for boundaries. Unfortunately, if you think such deficits in people are negotiable, you won't see them for the ingrained behavior patterns they are. When we focus on a partner's potential rather than their actual actions, we only see what we want to and make everything else fit.

At some point in a relationship, an EIP usually does something so distressing or rejecting that it cannot be explained away. Then you may feel incredulous or furious that the person is behaving so badly. This partner may have been letting you know for a while that things aren't going well, or that they're losing interest, but if you grew up with unsatisfying family relationships, you might not consider this a reason to pull back. Instead, you may fatalistically accept that relationships take a lot of work and are often unhappy. It may even feel heroic to persevere in unsatisfying relationships—the logical but erroneous conclusion of a childhood spent with a difficult EI parent.

But you have choices. Wouldn't it be easier to look for emotionally mature traits in potential partners from the very beginning?

Overall, sufficiently emotionally mature people like sharing happy attachments with other people and are neither overly dependent nor aloof. They are empathic and capable of putting others first when needed, but they maintain the rights to their own dignity and needs as well. They are adequately self-reflective and are interested in growth and improvement. They can certainly manage their self-esteem and emotional stability without your constant attentiveness.

Let's look at more specific ways to identify good partners and avoid emotionally immature ones.

Strategy

Ask yourself the following questions about a potential partner: Are they kind? Are they empathic toward others? Do they respect boundaries? When you talk, do they listen with interest? Do they give you feedback that shows they've heard your point? Do they remember what you say, and refer to it later? Are they fair and reciprocal? Are they good-natured over frustrations? These are just basic considerate behaviors, but an EIP will have trouble with them.

Respecting boundaries is an especially important characteristic. If you tell the person you don't want to do something, do they try to talk you into it? If you set a limit, is it accepted—or is it challenged? If they don't get what they want, do they get sulky or accept it gracefully? Do they make you doubt yourself by psychoanalyzing your choices? Do they act like they know you better than you know yourself? If so, that's not insight, that's domination.

When you talk, are they interested in how you see things, or do they double down on their own beliefs while dismissing yours? What happens when you have a disagreement or argument? Does the communication stay clear and direct between you, without becoming aggressive or insulting? Does the person seem to be trying to grasp your point of view, whether they agree with you or not?

Are they able to have fun? Do they add to your enjoyment of life? Do you find it energizing to be around them and do things with them? Are they enthusiastic about *your* dreams and ambitions? Do they accept what you need to be happy, even when it's different from their interests? And are they responsive to your bids for closeness, welcoming opportunities for these tiny moments of connection (Gottman and DeClaire 2001)?

Does the person have sufficiently mature coping mechanisms? For instance, do they have a sense of humor that takes the edge off life's frustrations? Do they take themselves with a grain of salt, or do they have to be right all the time? Does their temperament make them easy to get along with? Or do they become irritable, antagonistic, or uncooperative when they don't get their way? Can they be objective, flexible, and listen to facts, or do they become sarcastic and derogatory if someone disagrees? Do they manage their emotions well, or do they easily become angry or despondent?

What can you glean from their past relationships? Is there a lot of drama in their past? Is their life story full of villains? Are they still talking about how someone wronged them? Do they have a pattern of conflictual relationships or victimization? How well do they get along with their kids and coworkers?

Most of all, do you feel relaxed around them? Do you feel safe and seen in their presence? Can you be totally yourself around them? Do you sense that you can touch their heart and be understood when it really counts? Have you seen them under real stress? Would you admire how they handle things, even if you weren't dating them?

Although you may feel lonely or insecure at times, you are not an abandoned child in need of adoption, nor an undesirable person who should be grateful for anyone's attention. You are a self-sufficient adult in charge of auditioning people to become your *enjoyable* partner.

Reflection and Discovery

Think about a good relationship you had. It could be a best friend or a dating relationship. What were the person's qualities that made it so good for you?

_____

_____

_____

_____

Have you had close relationships in which you had to overaccommodate to make things work? Describe the ways in which you might have taken too much responsibility for improving the relationship, especially when the other person didn't show the same kind of accountability.

_____

_____

_____

_____

_____

Tip: Enjoyable partners can be very different from you—opposites do attract—but those differences should be complementary, not incompatible. To assess someone's emotional maturity, communicate your preferences and needs from the very beginning. Let them respond to the real you and see how it feels. Guard against any tendencies to be passive, put up a good front, or be overly accommodating of the other person. The relationship should feel easy and equal from the start, with both people showing sensitivity toward each other.

The *only* way to really get to know someone is to spend enough time with them to see how they handle stress and frustration. Take note, because that's how they might one day act toward you.

How do I make sure
I'm not an EI parent?

25

Knowing yourself prepares you for
emotionally mature parenting

Worrying about your children suggests you're probably *not* functioning as an EI parent because 1) you're thinking about them, so you're not primarily egocentric; 2) you're being self-reflective, taking responsibility for your parenting; and 3) you're being empathic toward your children's feelings.

If you listen to adequately mature parents talk about their children, it sounds like they're describing individuals whom they know in a well-rounded way, people with their own feelings and needs. In contrast, EI parents are more likely to describe their children's attributes piecemeal and superficially, focusing on their behavior, attractiveness, accomplishments, or problems, painting a parts-based "good" or "bad" picture of their children.

Your sensitive recognition of your children's experience is the foundation of healthy attachment between parent and child (Ainsworth 1982; Winnicott 2002). Sufficiently mature parents are interested in their children's unique personhood instead of expecting their children to mirror them. They also realize that their children need parental sensitivity and responsiveness, not just bodily care and protection.

When you've processed your own childhood issues, you are more likely to create a secure attachment with your own children. But if you deny the emotional truth of your past, it exerts a subconscious preoccupation that makes it hard to be fully emotionally present for your children. Suppressed or denied feelings make us less sensitive and empathic toward others, as we cut off access to those emotional experiences within ourselves.

As you compassionately review your own childhood experiences, you simultaneously build sensitivity and empathy for your own children. By processing how your parents' behavior affected you, you can define your own beliefs and priorities as a parent apart from what your parents did. The more conscious you are of how EI behaviors affected you, the less likely you will be to blindly repeat the patterns of the past.

Unfortunately, sometimes it's hard for us to resist old patterns from our childhood. Some part of you may remain entangled in old EI parenting models. Under stress, you might find yourself acting like your parents, getting angry at your children for insignificant things or feeling abandoned and hurt when they want distance from you. At other times, you might catch a glimpse of how you've hurt your children, but it's too late to take it back.

Since it's impossible for parents to be perfect, you may end up hurting or disappointing your children in ways that you might regret for years. But here's where the work you've done— reading, therapy, and self-reflection—pays off. As soon as you spot a lingering entanglement with old EI ideas and realize what you're doing—or have done—you can reverse course and make amends. If you regret some aspect of your parenting, think about why you acted that way. Were you insecure? Afraid for your children? Determined to be a "strong" parent? Think about how you wish you'd handled the interaction differently. If it feels right to you, address it with your children, even if it's years after the fact.

You can apologize to your children, tell them what you did wrong and how you wished you'd handled the situation instead. You can then listen to their take on your behavior and how you may have hurt them. By being a responsible person who has the integrity to admit when you're wrong, you increase their trust in you. Going back to your children and sharing your regret shows them how relationship repair is done.

With small or preverbal children, you may not be able to have the kind of discussion you can have with an older child, but you can still apologize and express contriteness. Your regret, facial expression, and desire to make up will communicate everything they need to know, along with a nice, healthy "I'm so sorry I hurt your feelings." You will be a model for them to do the same down the road. Your apologies are sowing a spirit of reconciliation that they will fall back on for the rest of their lives.

As children grow up and act like they no longer need you or insist that you stay in the background, you can remind yourself that they will never stop benefiting from your connection, encouragement, and interest. Pat yourself on the back when your child lets you know they need more room; you have a good enough relationship with them that they can speak up honestly. They don't see you as overly fragile or dependent on them for your self-esteem or purpose in life. When you are sensitive to feelings and show a desire for connection, you as an ACEIP can enjoy particularly close bonds with your children. It can be so different from what you experienced with your parents.

Now that we've discussed the all-important emotional factors in parenting, let's look at how you can become more mature in your parenting.

Strategy

Since EI parents are not the best models for desirable parenting, you can learn from parenting groups, parent coaching, or good parenting books. Seek recommendations from parents you admire, but make sure that the books you read support a parenting approach you can feel good about. Any book that endorses physical punishment, authoritarianism, or shaming will create more problems than it solves. Some helpful ones are *How to Talk So Kids Will Listen and Listen So Kids Will Talk* (Faber and Mazlish 2012), *Raising Your Spirited Child* (Kurcinka 2015), *The Explosive Child* (Green 1998), *How to Really Love Your Child* (Campbell 1977), and *How to Really Love Your Teenager* (Campbell 1981). It's also tremendously helpful to read up on child development so you can know what to reasonably expect from your child at different ages. It's easy to take childish behaviors personally, but you might feel differently if you realize that most children that age act that way. Consider reading the series of short books that starts with *Your One-Year-Old* (Ames and Ilg 1982) and progresses each year through preteens.

Reflection and Discovery

Think back to an incident in which you were particularly proud of your parenting. What happened and what did you do? Why do you think this memory is so satisfying? Did you give more guidance or empathy than you received as a child?

_____

_____

_____

_____

_____

_____

_____

_____

What are three things you've done differently in your approach to your children that may have helped reverse generations of emotionally immature parenting?

_____

_____

_____

_____

_____

_____

_____

_____

Tip: The simplest thing is to remember that children are people too. Look them in the eye and feel your connection together. They have the same sense of dignity and fairness that adults do. They feel things deeply and want to be good. They need empathy for their troubles, and for you to see their potential. Believe the best in them and collaborate with them to help them reach their goals. Give them guidance and encouragement, not just discipline. Help to mentally prepare them for unfamiliar situations, and afterward talk about what happened. Treat them with consideration and respect, as you would a fellow adult. These are some of the best gifts you can offer your children as an adequately emotionally mature parent.

Part III

Stepping Back

26

I can't help feeling guilty when they're upset with me.

Disengaging from the guilt of being yourself

Theresa told her mother, Mila, that she wasn't allowed to babysit Theresa's five-year-old son, Charlie, for a while. Mila had allowed Charlie to have unsupervised time with Mila's boyfriend even though Theresa had made it clear that she didn't want her son around him. It was a clear breach of Theresa's instructions about who was allowed access to her child.

Mila alternated between crying because she couldn't see her grandson and sulking because she felt Theresa was selfish and unreasonable for keeping them apart. This wasn't the first time Mila had overridden Theresa's wishes and tried to sneak things past her, but this time Theresa felt that she had to stop visits until her mother respected her wishes.

Mila neither apologized nor took responsibility for breaking Theresa's rule. Instead she acted righteously affronted, as though it should be up to her to decide if her boyfriend was safe for her grandson to be with. She argued with Theresa about her rule, instead of apologizing for breaking it. She insisted that as Charlie's grandmother, she had a right to see him.

When petulance and protest didn't work, Mila switched tactics and acted pitiful and abandoned, sending texts about how lonely and depressed she was, that life wasn't worth living if she couldn't have her family. Mila posed as the story's victim, done wrong by Theresa who didn't care about her feelings or even if she lived or died. Nowhere in all of it did Mila pause to consider Theresa's feelings or wonder if maybe she had crossed an important line.

Theresa saw through all of Mila's protests and held to her position. There was nothing about Mila's response that assured her she wouldn't do it again. She knew her mother had ignored her rules and had brought this situation on herself. However, Theresa secretly took Mila's accusations to heart and felt like a bad daughter for drawing the line. Theresa knew she was doing the right thing, but emotionally she felt terrible.

"What do I do about this guilt I feel?" she asked.

With the emotions of fear and shame, it's clear that the threat is coming from outside yourself. You know that the source of your distress is another person and how they're treating you.

But guilt is different, and in some ways it's more difficult to handle. There's irrational guilt and constructive guilt. *Irrational guilt* is little more than self-generated punishment for feeling like a "bad person." *Constructive guilt*, on the other hand, is a positive prompt to correct behavior and resolve a problem. Unfortunately, EI parents don't teach their children about constructive guilt and how to make things better. Instead, through guilt-tripping, they induce irrational guilt as a way of gaining more control.

Theresa's irrational guilt arose from her empathy for her mother. Even though Mila had caused her own distress, Theresa knew that her mother was upset, and she felt responsible for it. She was accustomed to being blamed by her mother and to feeling guilty for not being a better daughter.

Holding your boundaries when you feel irrational guilt may be one of the biggest challenges in relationships with EIPs. Even if you know you aren't responsible for their distress, you can still feel that way if you were led to believe that their moods are somehow your responsibility.

EIPs exploit your adult values of kindness and respect when they shift blame and induce guilt. You don't want to hurt anyone, nor do you want to think only of yourself. However, their accusations and exaggerated hurt feelings are designed to stir up self-doubt at an emotional level, even if you're very confident in your position. They weaponize your empathy and use it against you, inflaming your self-doubt by posturing as the victims of your insensitivity.

Theresa learned to step back from her irrational guilt. She began to anticipate her mother's projection of blame and victim posturing whenever she set limits. As Theresa stepped back, she recognized that her inevitable guilt feelings were an old reflex and stopped taking them so seriously. She realized that her guilt and self-doubt were coming from a child part of herself that still felt responsible for her mother's pain in life.

Let's look at some ways to manage irrational guilt when dealing with EIPs.

Strategy

Interrogate your guilt. When you find yourself doubting reality and blaming yourself, that's your cue to step back and question why you feel guilty. Perhaps you have an inner child part of yourself that feels guilty whenever someone seems unhappy. You can't let that confused, guilty child part run your life. You can understand the guilt, but you don't have to accept it. Challenge that self-blame reflex. You, the adult, are running the show, not your guilt-ridden child part from long ago. Ask those guilty feelings to step back and give you some room to think this through (Schwartz 1995, 2022).

Then ask yourself: *Did I do something wrong, or did I just displease them?* Think about where the guilt is coming from and if the EIP is somehow making their inconsiderate behavior *your* fault.

Reflection and Discovery

Think about a time when you felt guilty for setting a limit with an EIP. Describe the incident and the thoughts you had that made you feel guilty.

_____

_____

_____

_____

_____

_____

_____

_____

_____

_____

Try to pinpoint your guilt triggers: Exactly when in the process did the EIP point the finger at *you* for causing the problem? What exactly did they say or do that made you feel guilty?

_____

_____

_____

_____

_____

_____

_____

_____

_____

_____

Tip: If you feel guilty when someone is unhappy with you, pretend that the roles are reversed. If someone you cared about set a similar limit with you, how would you react? For instance, if someone told you that you'd done something that was affecting your relationship, and they asked you not to do that anymore, how would you respond? Would you accuse them of not loving you anymore? Of being ridiculous or selfish? Would you act wounded and give them the cold shoulder for daring to bring this up? I'm betting that instead you'd be concerned and try to work it out.

Feeling guilty is a trained reflex that once served the purpose of keeping you on the good side of people you loved. Being adequately mature doesn't mean you'll never feel guilt again. It means that you get to evaluate if your guilt is a childhood reflex or a legitimate concern.

I know they're acting crazy, but I don't know how to respond when they're being absurd.

How to spot and detach from EIP's projections and distortions

When EIPs become defensive, they can say and do absurd things. They won't hesitate to use illogical accusations and behavior at all costs to regain control of an interaction. It happens so quickly that you can't track the sequence of what they're saying. Let's slow it down and look at the five components that support absurd EI reactions.

EIPs see everything as either all good or all bad. The absolutist minds of EIPs make everything look black or white to them, all or nothing. Therefore, for them criticisms or complaints feel like sweeping repudiations of their worth. Threats to their self-esteem launch them into disproportionate defensiveness.

EIPs can't tolerate emotional intimacy. When you set a boundary with someone, you get real with them at a deeper level. Such honest sharing puts your relationship on more genuine footing, something EIPs can't tolerate for long.

EIPs are certain they're right. Remember, an EIP's reality is based on feelings, not facts. They *feel* innocent, so your complaint seems unfair. They can't believe that they could have overstepped or harmed you in any way. Since they didn't have malevolent intent, they're sure nothing bad happened. You are supposed to accept what they intended, not what it felt like to you.

EIPs cover their own mistakes by blaming you. For many EIPs, the best defense is a quick offense. They make you the guilty one, insisting that *you* have hurt *them*. If you confront them, they twist your words to prove they're unloved, misunderstood, or persecuted. This reinforces their life narrative of being the innocent victim of coldhearted villains (Karpman

1968). Their account of any conflict is like a Möbius strip visual illusion that's impossible to trace without ending up in utter bafflement.

EIP's emotions are highly variable. EIP's emotional states shift quickly, depending on whether they feel in control or threatened. They're always a hair's breadth away from seeing you as intent on hurting them for no reason. For instance, they might seem to recover from a disagreement or criticism, only to relitigate the whole thing the next day. Their moment of reasonableness evaporates as soon as they start thinking about how they're being persecuted again.

The following example illustrates how EIPs can shift toward absurdity.

David's mother, Marilyn, declared that she was coming for a visit on his five-year-old son's birthday in a couple of weeks, stopping by on her way to see an old roommate. Marilyn didn't ask for permission or if it would be a good time to visit. She also wouldn't give David an arrival time because she didn't like to be pinned down when traveling. Knowing his mother's unpredictability, David realized they could spend his son's whole birthday waiting for Grandma to show instead of doing something fun. So David told his mother that his son's birthday outing was going to be at two o'clock, and he hoped she could come but would understand if she couldn't be there in time. They'd leave a key so she could get in and rest after her trip.

Marilyn erupted. Now she knew they didn't want her to come. She clearly wasn't welcome. No matter, she was canceling the trip. She was no longer going to visit her former roommate either, the implication being that her son had devastated her so totally that she no longer had the heart to make a trip anywhere. She clutched at reasons to amplify her hurt and loss, even if she had to create them herself.

David was stunned by his mother's anger. He tried to reassure her that they weren't pushing her away, but she refused to listen and wouldn't return his calls. David was angry with his mother and her fantasies of persecution, and even angrier with himself for caring what she thought. All of it left him feeling guilty and frustrated. He had become entangled in her absurdities.

Marilyn rounded out this episode by calling a few days later and sounding chipper, as though nothing had happened. But then she called the next day to complain further about her mistreatment. David was astounded by the switches in her moods.

Upset EIPs are like three-year-olds who are just learning how to argue. Their arguments are barely better than tantrums. They know there's supposed to be a verbal back-and-forth, and they know they want to win, but beyond that they can't form a sensible argument because they can't think logically yet. Consequently, they demand to be right while saying whatever makes them feel empowered (for example, they're the injured one, it was someone else's fault, they didn't do it, you are being mean, it never happened, and so on). They construct reality to fit their story of being unjustly accused. They may lack logic, but they have perfect pitch for indignation, outraged posturing, and vitriolic accusations.

Fortunately, a week before his son's birthday David detached enough to regroup in the face of his mother's absurd behavior. Once David remembered that his son's birthday was his first concern—not his mother's hurt feelings—things fell back into place. He stepped back and saw everything clearly. He called his mother and calmly told her that his son was his priority, "above me, my wife, or you, Mom." His mother stayed home, his son had a great birthday, and David was proud of himself for reminding his mom of the realities. By refusing to rearrange his son's birthday around his mother's visit, David was honest with his mother instead of pretending to be fine with whatever she wanted to do. But for that moment of being genuine with her, he paid the price of her absurd allegations.

Sometimes you have to weigh the benefits of authenticity against the *energy costs* of standing your ground. For David, in this episode with his mother it was worth it; another time he might not have had the vigor to take her on. Don't feel bad if you give in when you're tired or stressed. If you push yourself to confront or set limits when you would rather withdraw or avoid, you'll get entangled with the EIP anyway because you didn't listen to yourself in the moment.

Strategy

When an EIP's behavior is approaching paranoia—absurd accusations not based on facts—you can either keep restating your position or back off if you're not sure of what you want to say. For example, at first David tried to steer his mother back toward reality. But when she devolved into blatantly absurd accusations, he withdrew and gave her space until he had clarified his intentions to himself. He realized it would do no good to argue, reason, or point out her distortions. She wasn't being rational enough for that to be effective. David turned his attention to thinking through his priorities and what he ultimately wanted to do.

Don't keep defending yourself against their blame. The EIP wants to fight so both of you are distracted from what they did. Instead, step back and detach from that senseless struggle and clarify your position. Go into observational mode, mentally labeling and narrating what they're doing as if you're slightly outside the situation. Pursue objectivity instead of reactive emotion.

Don't fall for the assumption that because someone is upset, you did something wrong. Although EIPs, just like toddlers, blame others when things don't go the way they want, it doesn't mean the blame is accurate. Emotional detachment allows you to see what they're trying to do: make you so miserable you'll give up and let them create the reality they want.

Reflection and Discovery

Think back on a time when an EIP took offense and got upset with you. Describe what they blamed you for or acted hurt by. Did it have something to do with doing things your way instead of how they wanted you to?

_____

_____

_____

_____

_____

How did you feel when you realized that their behavior was absurd? How did you feel when they distorted reality to support their accusations?

_____

_____

_____

Tip: Your job is to detach enough to realize that an EIP has become irrational. You may become aware that they're actually much weaker or more unstable than you realized. This realization can be painful because you've been groomed to see the EIP as a sane adult, even when their behavior is inappropriate or bizarre. But once you see through them, their absurdities will trigger objectivity and self-protection, not guilt.

I just want them to love me and understand my feelings.

Pick achievable goals instead

If you are an internalizer, you like being close to people, having meaningful conversations, and getting to know others better. You're happiest when other people reciprocate, building that bridge of friendship and closeness. In fact, this authentic, open approach is so satisfying that it's actually frustrating to dial it back to superficial social chitchat.

Like everyone else, you feel loved when someone takes an interest in you and wants to know more about you and your feelings. Unfortunately, when a self-preoccupied EIP ignores your subjective experience, you may try to build closeness by being even more open about your thoughts and feelings. You hope that increased openness about yourself might stimulate a closer relationship.

Your intent may be to spark interest, empathy, and engagement by moving the conversation into slightly deeper waters, but this outcome is not within your control. You cannot influence EIPs to be more empathic, nor can you make them be interested in you in the way that would make you feel truly seen and accepted. The more you try to spark that genuine connection, the more disappointed you may feel. You may struggle to connect, sharing your experiences, yet still end up feeling frustrated with how little you get back.

It's puzzling, I know, because you may sense that your EIP does love you and that you are important to them. You can feel the bond. They want a relationship even though their relationship behavior doesn't meet your criteria for real closeness. You know they're "in there," but you can't get them to drop their defenses and make the connection.

Yet every once in a while, you might have a spontaneous moment with an EIP, when they do show empathy and support in their own way. They might notice something about you and express concern, but they will probably lose interest if you try to explain your feelings. In other words, they occasionally may be moved to offer comfort, but it's when *they* notice it, not necessarily when you need it. Their brief supportive response is their way of saying that they care about you, but that doesn't mean they can talk about deeper feelings or help you with your experience.

Even when you're grown, you may still long for your EI parent to offer you a *holding* or *facilitating* environment (Winnicott 1989), just like you needed in childhood. This means that a parent has enough sensitivity and tenderness to create for their child a safely held space (that is, relationship) in which to grow and feel secure. Even after their children are grown, parents psychologically can still "hold" their adult children securely through their sustaining attention and emotional connection, and by offering empathy, support, and shelter from over-whelming circumstances. It's normal and healthy to want this kind of attentive relationship, as it gives us a safe space from which to grow.

We all have an intrinsic, lifelong instinct to keep maturing psychologically (Erikson 1950; Anderson 1995). We reach our fullest potential when our relationships support and encourage our growth. Perhaps you keep reaching out to EIPs close to you because you sense how enrich-ing it would be to grow with them in life through real sharing and mutual respect. As you mature, and especially when you start raising your own children, you might feel the natural urge to share your life journey with your parents. Their approval and empathy as you navigate new adult challenges would enable you to do your best possible job and to feel less alone.

But often this need for support creates goals that can't be met by an EIP. When EIPs feel pressured to give empathy or intimacy, they get irritable and introduce friction or disagree-ment to disrupt the closeness. Their irritable reaction to intimacy extricates them from engag-ing in something that probably makes them uncomfortable: getting emotionally close with people.

For instance, Ron called his elderly father to wish him a happy birthday. After listening to Ron's warm wishes, his father made a crude comment about Ron's preferred political party. Ron had reached out to his father with loving intent but was left feeling stung and angry. Ron had plenty of memories of his father doing this, deflecting a sweet moment with a crack that stirred up trouble. What Ron didn't realize was that while a thoughtful phone call might be something Ron enjoyed, his father was more comfortable being combative. A satisfying inter-action means very different things to different people.

Upon reflection, Ron realized that if he wanted to offer a warm gesture to his father, he needed to be ready for his dad's self-protective distancing. Not accepting this reality would leave Rob feeling upset while his father remained unfazed. Ron prepared himself for his father's reflexive rejection of closeness, and then stepped back and stayed neutral, no longer taking the bait of his father's barbs. When he led with warmth and openness, Rob wasn't going to get love or empathy; he was going to get his father's defenses. His father wasn't a growth facilitator but a closeness disrupter.

Just like Ron, you can read the waters and adjust your goals in relation to EIPs. Yes, your wish might be to have them love you and understand your feelings, but that goal may not be achievable. Because their reactions to closeness are so predictable, you might go ahead and express yourself because you want to, but be ready for their less than optimal response.

Now let's look at the importance of setting achievable goals so you don't get your feelings hurt as often.

Strategy

Expecting satisfying connections with EIPs can create a lot of emotional pain. The degree of the pain depends on the size of the gap between what you want and what you get. There's always the temptation to lead from the heart with anybody you care about, but this trusting openness may unwittingly prompt EIPs to pull back from you. Instead, try being more self-possessed, that enviable state where you collect yourself internally and know you will be all right regardless of other people's attitudes. If you set more achievable goals, such as simply expressing yourself or communicating directly without seeking deeper *emotional* connection, you have a better chance of feeling a sense of accomplishment. If you set your goal to have a single successful, self-possessed interaction instead of trying to build a close relationship, you might feel more empowered. You can set the achievable goal of planning your behavior, rather than hoping to elicit a satisfying response.

Reflection and Discovery

Think of a time when you missed an EIP and wanted to connect with them. How did it go when you reached out and tried to deepen your communication with them? How did you feel after talking with them?

_____

_____

_____

_____

_____

Looking back, what did you secretly hope to get from them? Write out your fantasy of how you wished they'd been. What exactly could they have said or done to make you feel satisfied and grateful?

_____

_____

_____

_____

_____

_____

_____

_____

_____

Tip: Practice self-possession and setting clear boundaries for yourself instead of seeking understanding and emotional support from EIPs. If you're aware of what you're dealing with and set realistic goals for engagement, you'll come closer to being happy with what you get. What you get may not be your idea of love, but it may be all they can give. Do you think you could accept this? Which way hurts less, having expectations for them or accepting their limitations?

Every time I set a boundary, I feel like a mean, heartless person.

When you feel guilty for protecting yourself

Narcissistic EIPs only feel loved when others mirror their wishes. Like very young children who get upset when someone says no, these EIPs' expectations of special treatment are challenged by your limit setting. How could you really love them if you want something different? They show their developmental immaturity and disregard for other people with their belief: *if you really love me, you will give me what I want.*

Boundaries are kryptonite to narcissistic EIPs. To feel existentially secure, they have to control you. It's unnoticed and immaterial to them that you have your own subjective consciousness and preferences (Shaw 2014). Your boundary reminds them that they don't rule you, threatening their sense of entitlement. They are terrified of becoming irrelevant if they don't call the shots and you don't put them first. When you claim your own boundaries, they see you as putting them down, undermining their sense of worth.

This is why in some relationships the narcissistic partner may become aggressive when their partner tries to set limits, threatens to leave, or withdraws love. This abrupt loss of privileged status sets off an existential panic, as if they are about to cease to exist. A psychologically fragile EIP, especially one with narcissistic features (Helgoe 2019), can become enraged and feel justified in taking extreme action to regain control. (Be sure to get professional advice and take necessary safety measures if you suspect that your situation may fall in this category.)

We usually think of narcissists as the grandiose types (Kernberg 1975; Kohut 1971) who have an inflated sense of self, but there are quieter, more covert types who wield power through guilt induction, passive aggression, or by emphasizing their unhappiness. These covert, passive narcissists (Mirza 2017), use stealthier pressures such as guilt, shame, gaslighting (Marlow-MaCoy 2020), silent treatment, and martyrdom, to name just a few, but the result is the same. Whether you fear an eruption or feel responsible for their depression or suicidality, you are being effectively controlled either way.

Whether narcissistic or not, EIPs are uninterested in the reasons for your boundary. They don't think their behavior is bothersome, so they think you should drop your complaints and let them continue on. Persistent attempts to explain will not induce them to listen because they're not self-reflective. To them, setting boundaries seems unnecessarily impolite, as if you're being cold and mean for no good reason.

Many ACEIPs imagine that when they finally set boundaries with an EIP, they'll feel self-confident and empowered. The sad truth is that you might feel like you failed. Instead of respecting your wishes, the EIP wears you down by showing resentment, insisting on what they want, or acting so hurt or angry that you wonder if taking a stand was worth it. They won't let you "win" with your boundary because they live in an all-or-nothing world in which cooperation, compromise, and mutual agreement are synonymous with losing. They don't grasp the concept of people listening to each other and reaching an understanding. You are either for them or against them.

In their mind, your boundaries are selfish. They don't care that you're trying to protect yourself or protect your rights to your own individuality. To them, they haven't done anything to you—except love you—and here you are ruining the relationship by being ridiculous. They don't see why you have to set limits because they're unaware of how their behavior affects people.

For instance, when one woman, Loni, set a boundary related to her mother's frequent attempts to run her life, her mother cried out in anguish, "Why are you doing this to me?!" Loni explained: "I'm not doing this to you. I'm reacting to you!" It's doubtful that this subtle distinction landed with her mother, but it was clear to Loni. She was not persecuting her mother for no good reason; she was protecting herself. Loni felt stronger once she stopped hoping her mother would understand her position. She realized that her mother didn't want a closer, more honest relationship—she wanted a daughter who was under her control. Loni also saw she wasn't being mean or heartless to her mother; she was just trying to be respected as a separate individual.

Let's now see how you might deal with similar situations and people.

Strategy

Maybe the best strategy is not compromise, but revolt. Not a revolt against the EIP, but a revolt against *your* trained tendency to let their demands make you feel bad about yourself. If you grew up with EI parents, a part of your personality may be standing by, ready to enforce guilt and shame even when you know better. After all, guilt and shame are the native currency of an entangled relationship with an EIP.

But when you feel that stab of indoctrinated guilt, telling you what a bad person you are for setting a boundary, remember that feeling so awful about yourself is never representative of the truth. Gain objectivity by labeling the EIP's judgment as a power play, and dispassionately observe how they try to inflame your self-doubt. Recall your sensible reasons for setting the boundary, then follow what your adult mind knows is best. As you're being criticized by an unreasonable EIP, remember that your worry about being mean and heartless is a good indicator that you've started taking care of yourself.

Sometimes EIPs get so defensive and accusatory that they'll cut off the relationship, trying to regain their absolute power. If they give you the cold shoulder or stop talking to you for setting a boundary, remember that all you did was act like someone who's an equal. Realizing the injustice of their rejection may help you prevent guilt. You can choose to keep trying to reach them, or you may decide to keep your distance. Their anger might be a sign that you are starting to live your own life.

Reflection and Discovery

Think about a time when you set an unpopular boundary with an EIP. What unspoken EI relationship rule did you break? Write out this old relationship rule as a statement, beginning with "It is wrong to…"

_____

_____

_____

Looking at this statement, what do you feel? How do you feel about living with this unfair rule up until now?

_____

_____

_____

_____

Now pick a healthier relationship value you want to follow. Put your new rule in statement form as well, also beginning with "It is wrong to…" Compare the two statements. Which one resonates more with you?

_____

_____

_____

_____

_____

_____

Tip: A difference of opinion doesn't make you heartless. Nor does declining something you don't want, or not putting an EIP first all the time. These could only be true if the greatest moral value in life was to keep this person happy no matter what—at your expense. The sign of your success is not that they accept your boundary, but that you set one. You protected your emotional health instead of letting them dominate you. You may even have saved the relationship from estrangement by making it bearable for yourself within reasonable limits.

They say I don't love them enough or in the right way. Am I capable of love?

Step back and assess what love is

If an EIP regularly portrays you as a selfish person who doesn't care about them, it starts to rub off on you. If, like most of us, you worry about what other people think, you may wonder if you've been unloving. Internalizers are open to learning from feedback, so you naturally wonder if there's any truth to such accusations. Both self-doubt and guilt get stirred up in these interactions.

You probably do love and care about this EI person—even when they unfairly accuse you of not loving them enough. They provoke you with their demands, and then when you show irritation they take it as proof that you didn't love them in the first place. This makes you worry that maybe you *are* coldhearted because you really *don't* like them when they do that. It's like when someone falsely accuses you of being angry; their unfair distortion actually makes you angry!

Complaints of being unloved are common with EIPs. It's their central wound and greatest fear. Perhaps something went wrong early in their life, making them feel unsafe and insecure. Perhaps fears around goodness and lovability make them worry that they won't be valued or taken care of. As a result, they're hyperalert to signs of untrustworthiness, infidelity of all types, or insufficient concern about them. Thanks to these suspicions, they often create the relationship problems they fear.

Many EIPs from emotionally deprived childhoods subconsciously seek emotional support from their children, safe people with whom they have very close bonds. This creates a reversal of roles, in effect parentifying their children (Minuchin et al. 1967; Boszormenyi-Nagy 1984). Not able to comfort themselves or maintain emotional stability, the EI parent expects their children to make them feel special and loved. It's a rude awakening for them when they discover that their babies and children are extremely self-absorbed by nature and demanding of constant attention. For the EI parent with insecurity issues, this normal childhood behavior is taken very personally, potentially plunging an EI parent into irrational feelings of being humiliated and dominated.

Inevitably EI parents act out their unresolved childhood needs and disappointments with their children. This explains some of the unfair expectations they've put on you. When their abandoned-child scenario is triggered, they see themselves as the innocent child and you as symbolizing their uncaring "parent." You can't love them enough now because they didn't feel loved enough back then. EIPs often try to reverse old emotional wounds with symbolic substitutes in their current relationships, but it cannot work. They will never feel loved enough to mend their insecurity and sense of unworthiness. Once you realize that you're being asked to make up for someone else's mistreatment from the past, you can reject these distorted accusations from the EIPs in your life.

Real love has room for both people in a relationship. Affection and acceptance should go both ways, so one person is not exploiting the other. It's not real love if one person takes control or demands proof of love through the other's self-sacrifice. You are the one who knows if you love an EIP, and you also know when you're giving until it hurts. When someone demands proof of love by expecting you to do something you don't want to, you're being treated as a possession, not a person.

Let's consider how you might handle an EIP's irrational accusations that you don't love them enough.

Strategy

When an EIP accuses you of not loving them enough or in the right way, take a step back and look at the big picture. You'll probably find that the behaviors that are making them feel "unloved" are about you defending your individuality or setting limits on how you want to be treated. Remember, loving them is not the same thing as giving them blanket permission to do whatever they want, nor is standing your ground a withdrawal of love. *They* are being unloving by criticizing your character because you needed to speak up for yourself.

Look at the power dynamics: are they communicating fair requests to you in a respectful manner, or are they making you feel bad so you'll submit to them? It's only when you step back far enough from the relationship that you can spot the difference.

You can reassure them of your love once or twice, but then you can refuse to discuss their accusations further. Even if you try to defend your perspective, they probably will remain focused on their emotional distortions. These distortions are not your fault, nor is it your responsibility to fix them.

Reflection and Discovery

Think about how you treat people who are important to you. Write a list of your interpersonal values—your guiding principles for interactions—that you try to adhere to in any relationship.

_____

_____

_____

_____

Looking at your list, do *you* think you have a capacity for loving others? How do you show caring? Look at your relationships across the years, then write about three memorable interactions that prove you are capable of loving others.

_____

_____

_____

_____

_____

_____

_____

Tip: As soon as an EIP puts you to the test regarding how much you love them, you know that person will never get enough love. Actually, "love" may not be the right word. Maybe it's more like they can't get enough of being put first, being allowed to dominate you, and being the innocent, injured party no matter what. When they challenge your love for them, it's a red herring enabling them to shirk the harder work of making sure the relationship is satisfying for *both* people. As you've probably noticed, such complaints have no solution. Even if you truly love them, you may never be able to "prove" it to them.

No matter what I do, they still seem hurt and betrayed.

Why your efforts to make EIPs feel better don't work

Many EIPs seem stuck in woundedness, long suffering, or betrayal. Something is always wrong. This is hard on you if you care about them—especially if you're their child—because your empathy is continually being depleted. The usual response to an unhappy person is to offer sympathy, which many EIPs rebuff, as if their troubles were too big to be softened by anyone's comfort. This dynamic is a catch-22: if you offer sympathy, it's too little and you're trivializing the depth of their distress, but if you don't try to comfort them, you're proving your lack of concern. You can't win. The only way you could satisfy them would be to constantly make everything about them.

You naturally want to help them feel better because that's what they seem to want. But the more invested you become in helping them, the more frustrated you may feel because of the intransigent negativity of their worldview. While you try to help them feel better about their current problem, they remain fixated on injustice, unfairness, and victimization, as if to affirm their disadvantage. They don't want help so much as they want you to validate their pessimistic outlook, which is that life is unfair and the deck is stacked against them. As soon as you offer objectivity and analysis, or don't agree that others are reprehensible, you may find yourself in the enemy camp too.

Unhappy EIPs don't necessarily want to feel better. They may just be seeking company in their unhappiness and bitterness. This is especially hard for internalizer ACEIPs to understand, because they tend to be problem solvers who want to help. Encouraging EIPs to get psychotherapy as a way of addressing the roots of the problem seems like a sensible idea, but they may be more interested in letting off steam than changing anything.

You also might suggest therapy because you're getting burned out listening to their complaints and nothing ever changing. You rightly sense that more self-awareness is what is needed, and you see therapy as a way to change the underlying patterns that keep causing problems. But if you suggest self-examination as a step in fixing any problem, EIPs will feel offended and criticized. Because they have an externalizing mindset, they only see how *other* people need to change. They keep trying to blame their way to a solution.

After a while, an EIP's self-defeating mindset can cause you to cut yourself off emotionally or withdraw out of self-preservation. You become desensitized to their unhappiness and outrage and feel for them less and less. You may withdraw your empathy because you realize it doesn't help to feel deeply for them. Nobody can sustain empathy when the other person continually presents themselves as martyr or victim. You get tired of putting out the effort while the EIP stays stuck in the same position.

What can you do about this frustrating dynamic? Here are some ideas.

Strategy

When an EIP is persistently negative, step back and assess what is really going on. What are they really asking for? Do they want your help, or are they looking for validation of their sense of oppression and injustice? Are they appreciative of your thoughts, or do they act like you don't grasp the magnitude of their suffering? Do they thank you for your support when they're feeling better, or do they move on to the next complaint?

Be on guard when their unhappy complaints are a result of externalizing blame and refusing to look at how they themselves could improve things. You can be kind and reassuring, but you don't owe it to them to wear yourself out with heroic efforts. A certain amount of healthy distance and skepticism is needed when a person complains and yet seems irritated or misunderstood when you offer help and suggestions.

Lastly, it's possible your sympathy and empathy aren't helping because there are deeper issues afoot that might come from the EIP's childhood mistreatment or deprivation. Your caring efforts can't reverse this early wounding because people themselves have to do their own work to recover from such serious mistreatment.

Reflection and Discovery

Describe an EI relationship that became draining because the person wouldn't accept feedback, yet continued to talk about the same problems. How did you feel toward them when they weren't interested in your thoughts or suggestions?

_____

_____

_____

_____

Can you think of another relationship in which you *have* enjoyed being empathic and helpful to the person when they have a problem? What's different about how this person talks to you? How are they different from the EIP in the way they respond to you?

_____

_____

_____

_____

_____

_____

Tip: If a person is mad at the world, consider not getting between them and their target. Is their mood your battle to fight, or your responsibility to fix? Do they want help, or are they pulling you down to join them in their depressing outlook? Ask yourself if you're mistaking their resentment and entitlement for actual emotional pain. If you feel defeated when trying to help someone, maybe they're invested in not changing. No matter how hard you try, your empathy and support won't change a person's underlying beliefs about the world. Only they can achieve that. You can still be kind without working hard to change their outlook. It's not necessary to give to the point of exhaustion.

I got free, but I miss our closeness.

When you feel sad about undoing the entanglement

When you step back from an entangled relationship with an EIP, you may be surprised to feel some sadness. Your annoyance with them may have obscured the secret gratification you've felt of being such a central person in their life. Missing the entanglement can be confusing if you expected to feel nothing but relief after successfully setting boundaries.

Don't forget that although it's freeing to become your own person, individuation means losing old relationship patterns. Stepping back can come with emotional costs that you didn't anticipate. There's bound to be a void when you stop putting the other person first. The part of you that used to revolve around the EIP is suddenly left with nothing to do.

You may have successfully set boundaries in the relationship before you had a strong enough sense of self to be comfortable with the change. You may feel slightly unmoored if your own self-development hasn't quite caught up to your individuation from that important person. Perhaps you never realized how much your identity and daily life revolved around the preferences of this person. However, you can catch up relatively quickly once you realize that the new style of interaction can be good for everybody.

Let's look at how this played out for my client, Avery, and her younger sister.

Avery was the only sibling of her depressed and alcoholic sister, Jill. After their neglectful single mother died when Jill was a teenager, Jill drank heavily and used Avery as her main emotional support person. Even after they became independent adults, Jill still expected Avery to call or text her every day. It wasn't unusual for Jill to call and complain of wishing she were dead or to stop speaking to Avery if she didn't show enough interest in Jill's problems. Avery felt as if she had two full-time jobs: supporting herself and worrying about her sister. Finally, it got to be too much, and Avery sought out coaching to help her set healthier boundaries with Jill.

With coaching, Avery began reflecting on how Jill's behavior affected her. As she stepped back and asked herself how she felt while interacting with her sister, she realized what it was costing her emotionally. She quietly began to define her own preferences before agreeing to what Jill wanted. Feeling that her emotional health was at stake, Avery pulled back and set limits on their contact. She also insisted that Jill get into therapy and find some new friends and activities.

Jill resisted. She already had the perfect support system in Avery! She was furious with Avery and, as she had done before, cut off all contact. As in the past, Jill expected Avery to keep calling her and to try to placate her. But this time Avery did nothing. Instead of worrying why her sister was not talking to her, Avery focused on herself and felt relief as she thought of new things she wanted to do with her free time. She felt less pressure and anxiety as she had more time to herself. She resolved to never again compromise her integrity just to keep the peace.

As if she had sensed Avery's individuation, Jill upped the ante and called Avery to say that she hadn't called because she had been suicidal, faulting Avery for not checking on her to make sure she was okay. Avery told her sister it was inappropriate to put the responsibility on her for monitoring Jill's suicidal tendencies. Jill argued that she should be able to count on her sister. Avery replied, "Jill, I will never do a mental health check on you again. I might call the sheriff to check on you, but I won't do it myself anymore. I will help connect you with someone who can help, but that's all."

Avery found this easier to say because she had stepped back and recognized the unfairness of Jill's willingness to traumatize her with threats of suicide. Through her actions and words, Jill showed that she was fine with Avery rushing to her apartment in a panic— thinking her sister was dying—yet considered the suggestion that she find a therapist preposterous.

When Avery held firm and maintained a healthier distance, Jill finally adjusted. She did find a therapist and began to take advantage of neighborhood opportunities for socializing and recovery. The real difference came when Jill got on medication and her mood lifted. With these other supports in place, Avery began to enjoy Jill's company more while continuing to meticulously check in with herself before agreeing to anything with her sister.

However, even after Avery had successfully set limits around her own life, she was surprised by how she continued to feel a strong pull within herself to call her sister and check on her. Avery subconsciously was afraid that neither she nor Jill would survive the individuation process. I reassured her that she wasn't killing her sister by living her own life. These were the pangs of an emotional separation that should've occurred years before.

Avery's emotional separation from her sister had outpaced her personal growth, so that she felt ill-equipped to deal with a life suddenly freed of so much responsibility. She had to update her self-concept as a person with her own life, rather than as an emotional support *for Jill and her problems. Avery decided to work on a healthier kind of relationship with her sister, in which she resolved to be honest, set limits, and not do what she didn't want to. To solidify her new self-concept, she thought deeply about her interests, dreams, and values as a unique person. As Avery turned toward her own growth, she began to feel more balanced and whole.*

Nevertheless, Avery continued to feel pangs at times: "I feel really, really sad, and homesick. I miss Jill. My emotional attachment to her was based on the emotionally broken sister that I had to hold together. My identity has been wrapped up in her brokenness all my life, and it was a very meaningful job. I was keeping her together; I was the first true, safe love my sister ever had in her life." Avery was grieving the loss of her essential role as her sister's emotional savior.

After a while, Avery began enjoying the freedom she had, now that Jill was functioning more autonomously: "I no longer feel that desperation, that urgency about her. Things don't feel like emergencies anymore." Looking back, Avery realized that in her previous relationship with her sister, she wasn't really loving—she was serving.

Let's see how you might handle similar challenges with EIPs in your own life.

Strategy

As you persevere in setting limits with an EIP, make sure you invest equal energy into discovering yourself and building a more accurate self-concept. Define the kind of relationship you want with them and articulate the values that you want to uphold in these new interactions. Ask yourself not only what you are trying to escape, but the changes you want to embrace.

Anticipate feeling loss or homesickness when this EI relationship changes or the person focuses their dependency on someone else. Perhaps you could write down two positive reasons to stay the course, if such feelings come up, to remind yourself of why these limits are important.

Reflection and Discovery

What are three interactions you currently participate in with an EIP but don't enjoy? (For instance, participating in activities you don't like, listening too long to them, hiding your real opinions, or agreeing with their expectations.) Are you being pressured to comply or do you go along from habit, or both?

_____

_____

_____

_____

_____

Imagine that you've stepped back and set healthy boundaries. Would some part of you miss the old interactions? Why? Name a couple of friends who might understand the paradoxical nostalgia of losing something that was not good for you. Keep them in mind as confidants with whom you could talk about this.

_____

_____

_____

_____

_____

Tip: Stepping back from an EIP lets you step back into yourself. But when you do, you might not recognize the place! Feeling awkward is understandable when you're not familiar with paying attention to your own needs. Remember, we all get very attached to accustomed interactions, even if they're harmful to us. The partial sadness you feel for the old days is unavoidable because you're a loving, emotionally connected human being. Accept the discomfort and weirdness that will be there for a while after you set limits. As you practice stepping back and conferring with yourself before agreeing to anything with an EIP, the process will feel increasingly natural.

Part IV

Saving Yourself

33

I traded authenticity for approval.

When being admired feels more important than being real

Most of us enjoy recognition and praise. The feelings they bring support our self-esteem and self-confidence. However, it becomes a problem if you work so hard to impress others that you lose touch with yourself. In your family you might have learned that over-striving for approval was needed because love and acceptance were highly conditional. If your EI parents fed on your success to satisfy their own self-esteem, you might have felt like you had to strive for both yourself and them. You might not have had a safe place where you could just be yourself. Perhaps you had to develop a pleasing persona to get along with others both inside and outside your family. Recognition from others might have felt like a psychological necessity. Consider the story of a gifted client of mine, Mike, who had such an experience growing up.

Mike went through a severe depression when he was in eighth grade, expressing his emotional state with goth clothing and dark poetry. His EI parents were always fighting and he wasn't fitting in at school. When he told his parents he was thinking about suicide, they took him to a psychiatrist who unfortunately prescribed a medication that worsened his depression to the point of a suicide attempt. In the aftermath, his parents told him they no longer knew what to do with him. They gave him an ultimatum: either he pulled himself together and stopped acting out, or they'd send him to a psychiatric hospital. Mike felt terrified at being banished from his family. He realized that the only help available had to come from himself.

Therefore Mike started high school with a new mission: he would become the high achiever his parents wanted. He started dressing in conservative, preppy clothes, joined the track team and drama club, and studied hard in advanced placement classes. He was trying to qualify as lovable by appearing as normal and successful as possible. Mike had the intelligence and ability to pull this off, and his parents seemed proud of him.

Mike's strategy brought him positive attention from adults and allowed him to fit in with supportive groups at school. He had successfully hidden his sadness with a mask of achievement. However, Mike's unresolved depression and basic insecurities went underground, only to resurface in adulthood when a relationship breakup left him feeling desperate again. To regain his balance, Mike had to learn to be authentic about his feelings instead of chasing praise and acting like everything was fine. He realized that securing his parents' approval had cost him his emotional health and had disconnected him from his real feelings.

Not everybody would attempt such an extreme "solution" of trying to make themselves into another sort of person entirely, but such self-eclipsing attempts at transformation probably happen more often than we realize. We all perform mini-versions of approval seeking when we suppress our authentic reactions and opinions so as not to alienate those upon whom we're emotionally dependent. This is especially true with EIPs since they can be so rigid and judgmental about acceptable appearance and behavior.

When you live up to other people's expectations to the point of losing yourself, your adaptation has gone too far. Too much of this can lead to isolation, low self-esteem, and depression. Like Mike, you might not foresee the long-term effects of so much approval seeking, including how it undermines relationships.

When you feel like you need to impress others, it makes it hard to relate at a more authentic level. It's hard to feel close to anyone if you see them as someone you need to impress. Even though you may no longer be surrounded by EI family members, you may still stifle your authenticity for fear of other people's rejection. When you fear that other people won't like what you have to offer, you may start presenting yourself as what you think they value. If you habitually seek worth through approval, it becomes increasingly hard to interact as your real self.

So how do you go about being more genuine and less fixated on approval, not only with EIPs but with everybody?

Strategy

You can catch yourself chasing approval by noticing whether you're feeling energized or depleted during an encounter. You'll feel tense as you struggle for admiration and monitor whether other people are looking up to you. Use this tension as a signal to take a deep breath and feel your own worthiness just as you are. See if you can interact as a regular human being, not as someone trying to ace an audition. This of course will be much easier as you spend more time with people who are not EIPs.

You could start becoming more authentic by offering your true opinion, even if it's different from that of others. Instead of figuring out what everyone else thinks, why not go ahead and share your ideas in a neutral, friendly way? You don't have to push or defend your point of view because you're just participating in a conversation. Authenticity is more doable when you practice it a little bit at a time in social interactions with safe and accepting people.

Experimenting with more authentic responses lets you get accustomed to letting people see more of the real you. Not everybody will be a critical EIP. You may still enjoy approval, but your deeper goal can be to get along with other people *and* get along with yourself. As you show more of your real self to others, you can enjoy friendships and relationships in which you don't feel so on guard.

Reflection and Discovery

Write about a time when worrying about approval got in the way of you being yourself with someone. What did it feel like to be so concerned about how they saw you that you couldn't be yourself?

_____

_____

_____

_____

_____

_____

_____

Make a list of personal qualities you see in yourself that are just as important as your accomplishments. If you struggle with this, consider the sort of characteristics you find attractive in a friend. If it's still hard to see your good qualities, ask a friend to give you some feedback. By doing this you'll build a more realistic self-concept that includes all of you, not just your achievements.

_____

_____

_____

_____

_____

_____

Tip: Your desire to be admired may have caused you painful moments of inauthenticity, but instead of concentrating on making a good impression, you can try to be genuine in a friendly way. You're just setting a different goal. It's okay to seek recognition, but not at the expense of your genuineness. Start seeing yourself as someone who not only likes approval, but also wants authenticity and closer relationships. See what happens when you don't try so hard to be exceptional. Start slow and experiment in little ways that only you may be aware of. You have the perfect right to feel worthy and valued just for being yourself.

34

I want to be myself,
but I fear rejection.

Handling the anxiety of abandonment

Human beings have competing needs for individuality and belongingness. Most of us are familiar with this balancing act of wanting our space but needing relationships too. In the best relationships, we get to have our individuality and boundaries, while still enjoying shared closeness and attention.

But in relationships with EIPs, this balancing act often fails. That's because the EIP, with an underdeveloped sense of self, has trouble sensing where the healthy balance should lie between individuality and belonging. They veer too far over the line both ways, making other people feel either emotionally isolated or overly controlled, or both. They don't know how to find that happy middle ground where people can fully be themselves yet share supportive closeness.

Sufficiently mature relationships require people to honor each other's autonomy and inner psychological world. But EIPs are stuck at a developmental stage where they see others as extensions of themselves or as objects for their own gratification, with little empathic awareness of their needs. Like toddlers, they can't grasp the idea that other people are meaningfully separate from them with minds of their own.

You can imagine what happens when toddler children of EI parents begin to express their individuality and autonomy apart from their parents. There's no way EI parents can graciously accept this necessary developmental step. Instead they take their children's independent efforts as a personal rejection, seeing them as willful or rebellious. They might react emotionally by pulling away from their children, temporarily depriving them of the home base they need for emotional comfort and reassurance. This teaches their children to fear seeking independence because it might lead to loss of connection, to abandonment, or worse. Children who are put in this position face an impossible choice between developing their own identity or keeping their parents' love.

EI parents hold full power over their children. Parental support is a matter of survival to children, for there is no place else for them to go. This is where many of the panicky feelings that ACEIPs feel come from. The possibility of being rejected by your source of security is

terrifying for anyone, but especially for young children. If you felt such insecurity in childhood, you might dread being dropped or rejected if you get too full of yourself. An underlying
terror of rejection can last into adulthood, explaining why many ACEIPs seem irrationally
panicky if a significant EIP turns cold or cuts off contact.

For instance, Jamal struggled to stand up for himself in his relationship with his authoritarian father, Otis. As Jamal put it, "Around him I have a hard time being the person I want
to be." Otis constantly gave Jamal unsolicited advice, until one day Jamal finally set limits
with his father.

> *When Jamal let Otis know he needed to make his own decisions, Otis was furious and
> stopped speaking to him, punishing Jamal for asserting himself. Although Jamal was finally
> getting the space he wanted, he couldn't enjoy it because he couldn't stop worrying about
> Otis's withdrawal. He was surprised at how insecure he felt knowing his father was mad
> at him.*
>
> *Now he understood what had been preventing him from setting limits with Otis
> sooner. The consequences were so painful! Jamal felt the urge to apologize profusely and
> beg his father not to be mad, but he managed to resist these panicky reactions. He decided
> to occasionally reattempt contact with Otis until he became receptive again. Jamal learned
> that his world didn't collapse when Otis withdrew his love and that he could withstand
> some acting out on his father's part in order to have healthier boundaries later. In Jamal's
> words, "A shift has occurred toward my dad. I see him differently, I see his limitations.
> Before, I thought it was 'incidents' we went through, but now I see it's his personality
> pattern. This is who he is, and I really don't like it."*

Adequately emotionally *mature* parents consistently welcome their growing children back
to the nest even after they've rebuffed their parents' attention and insisted on going their own
way. This kind of parent understands such irresistible urges for freedom and self-efficacy.
They realize their importance as an emotional refueling station for their young children,
allowing them to go out and come back at will, always certain of their parents' welcome
(Mahler, Pine, and Bergman 1975). For autonomy to feel enhancing and not scary, children
must know that their parents will be there when they need them again. Children treated this
way can feel self-expressive, exploratory, and cared about all at the same time. Self-discovery
doesn't result in a loss of love.

But if you had EI parents, old childhood fears may make you worry that their displeasure—or that of others—will lead to your abandonment. Fortunately, since you are an adult

now, you have many options for other sources of support. Even though it may feel like it, you're no longer dependent on that parental approval for your security.

Here's what you can do if you fear being abandoned as you become more genuinely yourself.

Strategy

Recognize and comfort that part of yourself that fears abandonment as the price for your independence (Schwartz 1995, 2022). Listen to that part's fears and write them down, but then ask yourself how *you* would like the relationship with the EIP to be going forward. Though your anxiety may make you want to jump back in and beg forgiveness, think about how much contact—and what type—you really want.

When you feel punished or emotionally abandoned by someone who reacts poorly to your autonomy, immediately clarify for yourself your values about how you think people should treat each other. Remembering your values helps you rise above an EIP's backlash and get perspective instead of worrying about guilt or abandonment. Instead of reacting, assess their behavior. Do you think it's fair to treat others like they're contemptible if they disagree with you? Do you think it's okay to emotionally abandon loved ones when they don't give you what you want? Instead of automatically feeling guilty about "causing" your own abandonment, evaluate how you're being treated and seek emotional support from someone more caring.

Now let's further clarify your values around your right to be an individual.

Reflection and Discovery

How much freedom do you think people should have to set limits on the amount or kind of contact they want with others, particularly EIPs? Would a person be wrong to ask for less contact if they didn't enjoy the time spent together?

_____

_____

_____

_____

_____

Think about how it feels when EIPs use emotional withdrawal or threats of abandonment to make you spend more time with them than you want. Review your values and write a position statement on your views about this kind of pressure. Where do you stand on this type of behavior?

_____

_____

_____

_____

_____

_____

_____

Tip: It's possible that an EIP might keep up the silent treatment indefinitely if you establish boundaries with them, but it's more likely that after a while, when their mood shifts, they'll contact you as if nothing happened. (It's astounding that EIPs can act as if everything's normal after they've behaved atrociously.) Your instinct as an emotionally connected person might be to try to resolve the issue that led to the break. If you like, you could ask them if they'd be willing to talk about it, but you also have the option of dropping it as well. You might prefer to stick politely to your new boundaries and rights of expression, without trying to get them to understand the hurtful or punitive effect they had on you. The important thing is to know what kind of relationship you want to have now, and to steer your actions by that goal.

Who am I really? How do I know for sure what's best for me?

How to recognize your true self and restore your authenticity

Emotional coercion and takeovers by EIPs can make you feel like more of a set of reactions than a person in your own right. When you worry too much about what other people want, it may seem like your inner voice has stopped talking to you. You may lose touch with your own preferences or even who you really are at your deepest level. How can you go about finding and reconnecting with your true self?

To reconnect with the core of yourself, notice when your energy rises and falls. Look for what fascinates you and follow your interests. When you pursue things that are right for you, you'll have a sense of expansion and meaningfulness. Time passes quickly, and while your activity may be hard work, it's energizing and uplifting. As you engage with your true interests, you feel like you're in the right place at the right time, and the next steps follow along nicely.

Think about the genuineness of healthy children before they've been taught to cover up their feelings and think about their actions. They have great energy because they're not in any internal conflict. They're comfortable in their bodies, open with other people, and ready for the next thing. They are guided from within by what they like and don't like, and they feel safe sharing their emotional truth with people they love. Locating your true self involves noticing your dreams, feelings, and impulses when you're totally being yourself—as most children do naturally.

If you've ever interacted with someone while feeling connected with your true self, you probably remember the moment. In these moments you're in a hyperpresent, unthreatened, self-possessed state of mind in which you feel calm, think clearly, ask questions naturally, and correct misperceptions nondefensively. When you're centered in your real self, there is no brain scramble or loss for words—even when talking with an EIP—because you feel little to no anxiety. Instead of feeling self-conscious, you're fully present. You are quietly confident and there's no internal struggle. Words and ideas come to you from a deep inner sensibility, and you can tell what's true and what's not. Above all, there is a sense that no matter what happens, everything will be all right because you're in the right frame of mind to handle it. Feeling firm, yet peaceful, you see the heart of the matter and move forward without ambivalence.

Your true self speaks with a still, small voice that guides you toward things that enhance your life energy and support your essential individuality (Gibson 2020). If you fight this inner guidance, you can produce internal conflicts so strong that they can cause symptoms. For instance, we become anxious when we deny our true wishes, and we become depressed when we think there's no hope for being our authentic selves.

So where is this true self when you really need it? You know, like when you're struggling with an EIP's domineering or coercive behavior? It's still there, but it gets hidden as your defenses step in. The solution is to stay connected to your self from the beginning of an EI interaction rather than losing the connection after being triggered and then trying to find it again. So, if possible, take the necessary moments to center yourself *before* you have a significant interaction with an EIP. When your true self is leading the rest of your personality, you'll be calmer and much less reactive (Schwartz 1995, 2022).

Your true self is the foundation of your entire personality, and it has been there since your beginning. It's always there if you remember to look for it. Part of the popularity of meditation and mindfulness is that these practices take you into the spaces where the true self lives, where you can connect with your own depths.

As you tune in to yourself, your true self will emerge more often in your interactions. You'll know what you really think, how you really feel, and what you do and don't need from others. It always amazes me how some people, after reconnecting with their true feelings, spontaneously start speaking the truth to EIPs simply because it's so much easier to just say what needs to be said rather than quash it. When you're in touch with your true self, the right words come out. Let's look at an example.

> Shanice's mother, Imani, liked to babysit Shanice's young children. But Imani ignored Shanice's instructions, feeding the kids the wrong things and letting them stay up late watching TV with her. Multiple confrontations did little good because Imani insisted there was no harm in spoiling one's grandchildren. So when Shanice and her husband took a weekend trip, Shanice asked her in-laws to babysit instead. When Imani demanded to know why the kids were staying with the other grandparents, Shanice decided to tell her the truth: "We're going to leave the kids with them because they're very deferential to how we want things done. Those kids are my responsibility. Until I know they're getting what they need, I'm not leaving them with you."

So how did Shanice find these words? She'd done the work of being deeply honest with herself about what she did and didn't want. She was able to speak the truth about her position to her mother because she was absolutely clear about what was right. You can do the same when you discover *your* self.

Strategy

So who are you? Like Shanice, you are that calm core inside you that knows what it prefers, is clear about its needs, and reacts to life authentically.

In order to experience your true self, try making a special point to get quiet and center yourself meditatively. By taking some comfortable breaths with the intention of connecting with yourself, you can get a sense of who you are underneath your various roles. It's already in there, that very aware inner consciousness that knows what's good or bad for you.

Your true self lives in quietness, awareness, and calmness (Schwartz 1995). Meditation, mindfulness, journaling, therapy, or deep conversations with a trusted friend can reconnect you with the essence of your true self. There are easily accessible meditation apps (for example, Headspace, Calm) and resources online, or you can search out introductory meditation books that appeal to you either online or in bookstores. You can use these resources to clarify what appeals to you and what makes you feel energized and alive.

When you're faced with a difficult challenge, you can get quiet and ask yourself, *What is the most essential truth about myself and this situation?* Try doing this with pen and paper, writing down more and more truths about what's going on, what you feel, and what you value.

Who are you? This question is answered in those moments when you're so fully yourself you forget to ask that question.

Reflection and Discovery

Take some time to sit down and think of a time when you felt aligned with your true self. Write about where you were and what this experience felt like.

_____

_____

_____

_____

_____

If you feel disconnected from your authentic self, write about when and how that shift occurred. What events or people took you further away from your true self? Which influences connected you more with it? Write down what these answers tell you about what you need more or less of in your life.

_____

_____

_____

_____

_____

Tip: The demands of EIPs can disrupt your connection to your true self. They put themselves between you and your deeper inner world, drawing your attention to them and taking you out of harmony with yourself. But as you look past them, seeking out the truth of your own experiences, your true self becomes brighter and more accessible to you. It is only through this improved communication with your true self that you find out who you really are and what you want. When you take time to reconnect to your underlying self-awareness, you begin to remember who you've been all the time, long before EIPs pressured you to ignore who you are so as to better attend to them.

I try so hard to do things perfectly that I exhaust myself.

When your self-esteem is based on doing the impossible

Perfectionism can be a problem for internalizer ACEIPs. Their heightened perceptiveness and sensitivity make them notice things that others may overlook, especially visual details and people's reactions. Perceptiveness and perfectionism can be applied toward achievement, but these sensitivities also make internalizers painfully aware of other people's displeasure. As a result, they set the bar as high as possible for themselves, not only because they want to do a good job, but because they want to forestall any possible criticism.

Are you perfectionistic? Are you so critical of your efforts that it's hard for you to get started, even on projects you're interested in? Is your self-assessment colored by feelings that you won't measure up to what others find praiseworthy? If so, you know that perfectionism doesn't let you enjoy the pleasure of "flow"—of being immersed in whatever you're doing. Perfectionism bleeds the fun out of everything.

When you become your own worst critic, your response to your best effort is immediately and painstakingly to find everything wrong with it. This can be demoralizing. Plus, finding mistakes is a process that feeds on itself, making everything look like it needs correcting.

You become your own worst critic after you've been repeatedly evaluated by other people. EIPs externalize blame and criticize others, so their children often feel like they're being compared to a standard of excellence they can never reach. Even when you try your hardest, you inevitably miss something and feel shame. Unfortunately, many EI parents have more aptitude for criticism than for being helpful or supportive. By reacting with evaluation rather than delight, the message is always that you could've tried harder. EIPs just can't resist making themselves feel more competent at your expense.

Critical EI parents seem to think it's their children's job to *impress* them, rather than for them to encourage their children in their efforts. This pushes children to overachieve, trying to be remarkable enough to win their parents' elusive approval. Such parents lack the empathy to see that their children need to take pride in what they've done. They are too focused on their children's output to notice their feelings. As a result, sensitive children become overly cautious, avoiding shame by being so careful that no one can fault them.

Children instinctively notice who has power and try to copy their behavior, and this learned behavior is integrated into how internalizer ACEIPs navigate life. For example, at work you might copy an EIP's critical attitude toward you to beat them to the punch. You may tear your work apart before giving them the opportunity. You may believe that overextending yourself is the minimum required for a sense of self-worth. Taken to an extreme, you might become hypercritical toward your own personhood. Criticism doesn't stop at the boundaries of your work; it travels upstream to the source of your self-esteem, your sense of self.

Perfectionism makes for an ideal servant but an awful master. If it were saved for the final touch-ups on a project, such scrutiny might help. But perfectionism knows no limits, preempting creativity to *prevent* mistakes instead of being invited in later to correct them. And when you try to prevent all mistakes, pretty soon you're producing nothing at all.

Although misguided, your perfectionistic part is just trying to keep you safe (Schwartz 1995, 2022). It learned that caution and self-criticism were better than waiting for someone to puncture your enthusiasm. It's only trying to protect you by getting everything right from the very beginning.

Because perfectionism is based in black-and-white opinions, impatience, and unrealistic standards, we can see that it's a form of EI thinking. Like EIPs, your perfectionistic part is impatient because it doesn't want to "waste" time doing rough creative work. It expects to arrive at the right answer before you've tried anything. But what perfectionism haughtily calls a "waste of time" is actually the EI problem of low stress tolerance.

Just like an EIP, your irrational perfectionistic part doesn't want the suspense of seeing how things turn out; it wants it polished before you begin. Like EIPs, perfectionism gets things backward, demanding that reality should match fantasy. It denies that the slog of creating usually has false starts, dry runs, and many, many corrections. It insists that you should be able to forego all that stress and messiness. It rejects reality in favor of the grandiose fantasy that doing something perfectly the first time is actually possible.

Let's look at some ways to work with your perfectionism to make it less self-defeating.

Strategy

Dealing with a perfectionistic part of yourself can be just as exhausting as dealing with an irrational EIP. Perfectionism is similarly impatient, unrealistic, and unreasonable. Try communicating with your perfectionistic part, as if it's a separate person. Ask it what it's trying to do by being so relentlessly critical so early in the process (Schwartz 1995, 2022). You might find out that it doesn't trust you to remember how humiliating it is to be exposed for mistakes.

As you engage with this part of yourself—listening to its fears and acknowledging its attempts to save you from shame—you may be able to form an alliance. Perhaps its laser-like discernment can be brought in at opportune moments instead of at every step of the way.

For instance, what if you and your perfectionistic part teamed up, but with sharply divided stages to supervise? What if you gave yourself a criticism-free period of time in which to tackle a task and get a rough approximation done before you invited perfectionism to participate? Or what if your self-evaluative part was allowed to participate, but only in an encouraging or curious way, such as by creatively puzzling over how to make something even better, rather than slamming it with wanton criticism. Ask your perfectionistic part to step back (Schwartz 1995, 2022) and let you experiment and create before you submit your work to it for quality review. With this new approach, you could end up with something that you really like—not perfect from the start, but full of life from the beginning.

Reflection and Discovery

Describe the kind of activities that tempt your perfectionism. Then, put your perfectionistic part's motive into words. What humiliating outcome is it trying to avoid (for example, *If this isn't perfect, then…*)?

_____

_____

_____

_____

_____

_____

_____

_____

_____

Contemplate an embarrassing incident from childhood when an EI adult made you feel small or inadequate. Write about the impact this childhood event had on you. Then, referencing your current adult values, write down how you feel about an EI adult making a child feel so self-conscious. Do you want to keep treating yourself that way with your own perfectionism?

_____

_____

_____

_____

_____

_____

_____

_____

_____

Tip: Perfectionism is fueled by traumas related to feelings of unworthiness. It usually comes from a young part of yourself that's trying to overcome deep fears about not being sufficient. This young part doesn't realize that life's goal isn't never to make mistakes; it's to learn from the mistakes you do make. Your perfectionistic part may be trying to produce something of quality, but it just jumps into the mix too early. Perfectionism shouldn't be allowed to run the show; unleash it only when it's time for it to play its part.

I wish I weren't such a people pleaser.

When you trade being yourself for being liked

I always wince when people disparage themselves for being people pleasers. It feels like such an unfair self-diagnosis. I can guarantee you that no child would become a people pleaser if they felt like they could be themselves and still feel safe and loved. People pleasing is a survival skill, not a moral weakness. To use the term as self-criticism is really blaming the victim. You probably learned that people pleasing was the price of belonging.

People who consider themselves people pleasers often criticize themselves for trying too hard to maintain good relations with others. If this is you, you're familiar with the internal battle between the part of you that wants to please and the part of you that wishes you were more genuine. Pulled between these two sides of yourself, you end up with a conflicted self-image. Part of you likes it that you are socially skilled and able to get along with most people, while an inner purist accuses you of selling out.

Because you feel torn between pleasing others and being honest, it may feel like you have to choose between being self-effacing or confrontational. But really, you wouldn't be happy with either side taking over. How do you get along in the world if you forego your tact and social skills? And where would you be if you weren't honest enough with other people? We all need the courage to be aware of who we are, while tempering our self-awareness with the sensitivity to think of others too.

Being liked is not the same as being a sellout. Pleasing others is a set of skills heavily dependent on several things: empathy, perceptiveness of other people's reactions, and a taste for harmony over chaos. Many of us picked up these skills within our families, ACEIPs in particular as they helped EIPs manage their emotions, behavior, and self-esteem. We noticed what raised people's spirits, and which irritants started a bad mood. This instinct to please develops early, operating unconsciously and automatically, helping us to make any atmosphere feel a little less toxic.

If this was you, you may have learned early how to soothe your parent, trying to be the kind of child who never gives their parents a moment's trouble. Instead of thinking for yourself, you may have felt like nothing was more important than going along with what the EIP wanted. This feeling is the result of being pressured to psychologically fuse (Bowen 1978) or enmesh with the family (especially the parents) and not differentiate into your own individuality.

Your parent-pleasing role then became the backbone of the parent-child relationship, and you might have been afraid to let the mask drop for fear that without it there wouldn't be any relationship at all. This pleasing *false-self* (Winnicott 1989) was originally created to channel your parent's love and approval, but now you may find yourself using it with everybody.

It's important to your self-esteem to know that when you overaccommodate people who make you nervous, you're acting on instinct for a very good reason. You may have learned that pleasing others or worrying too much about what they think is the safest way to go. What makes people pleasing feel bad is knowing that fear motivates your pleasing, not just social skill.

I just want to emphasize that of course you respond out of fear! If you grew up with EIPs, you know how reactive and insensitive they can be. It was a smart thing for you as a child to develop these instinctive, placative defenses to help calm and manage them. You learned people pleasing in order to make your life easier and safer back then. Even though now as an adult you may be much better able to handle difficult people and set boundaries, when that inner scared child takes over, you might revert to a powerless kid who can't speak up.

Your job now is not to stop being a nice or pleasant person; it is to stop *detaching from yourself* in the process. The first thing a psychological defense like people pleasing does is to hide your true self. A coping mechanism's only purpose is to deal with outside threats, not consider what you want or who you are. Your task now is to understand that these people-pleasing defenses are self-protective, automatic responses from childhood, and then use your adult mind and true self to redirect them. Now you can consciously employ the skills of people pleasing when it's to your advantage, but without detaching from your true self. You know how to be likable; now you can repurpose that skill to be effective on your own behalf in your adult life.

As an adult, it is now your choice when you want to use your people-pleasing skills. You might feel it's advantageous to please others sometimes, but not at the cost of hiding your true self. Now you can consciously tell the difference between your inner experience and what others expect you to be. You don't have to be entangled with them. You are your own person.

Now let's look at how you might decline to make everything about the EIP's feelings and become more authentically yourself.

Strategy

The first step in being more authentic is to become more aware of your own reactions and feelings while with other people. If you maintain that conscious inner connection to your own self, you can disagree with someone while still using your people-pleasing skills to get along with them and keep things comfortable. The important thing is that you also practice feeling present and aware during all interactions, so that your old self-erasing instincts are not dictating your responses.

Go into every EIP interaction with the conscious intent not to detach from yourself. So you don't lose touch with yourself, make a point to focus on your breathing and body sensations as you interact with the EIP. Tune in to the center core of yourself and practice being consciously present throughout the interaction. Be self-possessed and don't allow yourself to go on autopilot. Silently talk to yourself. Think about what they're saying but stay aligned with your true reactions.

Have a grab bag of noncommittal responses ready ("I see," "Hmm," "Okay") so you don't lapse into reflexive enthusiasm for things you might not agree with. Instead of automatically agreeing with whatever they say, pause and say, "That's interesting," giving yourself a moment to clarify your genuine opinion. Then you could say, "I have a slightly different take on that. I was thinking that…"

Cutting back on people pleasing doesn't mean everything has to be a confrontation. As long as you know how you feel, and what you like or don't like, you will have a connection to your true self. When you maintain a conscious connection to what you really want and the outcome you desire, you won't people please yourself into inauthenticity. If you want to be nice as you move toward that goal, that's your choice, as long as being nice doesn't put the urge to please back in charge.

Reflection and Discovery

What do you fear might happen if you didn't work so hard to get people to like you? How does that worry relate to circumstances earlier in your life?

_____

_____

_____

_____

_____

Remember a time that you were with someone who activated your people pleasing, so that you became inauthentic. If we could pause the moment and ask you why you felt like you had to please them, how would you explain it?

_____

_____

_____

_____

_____

Tip: You can choose to be likable, yet not compulsively feel that you have to be liked in order to be accepted as a full human being. As long as you don't disconnect from yourself in the other person's presence, you have accomplished the most important goal. You can always use your likability skills, just as long as you know you're using them and they're not a sign that you've forgotten about yourself.

38 It kills me to ask someone for help.

Why you apologize and feel like a bother

If it's hard for you to ask for help, you're in good company. For many ACEIPs, asking for help feels like an unwarranted imposition on other people's time and good nature. They assume helpfulness in others is in short supply and thus resist drawing on it. Consequently, many ACEIPs won't ask for help if there's any possible way to take care of something themselves.

EI parents, through their behavior, teach their children that other people are overwhelmed with their own problems and don't want to be troubled with the burdens of others. They probably don't intend to make their children feel bad for needing help, but their self-centeredness and low stress tolerance means that they often see their children's issues as hassles. Many get so absorbed in their own lives that they forget how vitally important their emotional support is to their children. They don't think about how crucial their attention is, nor how much their annoyed reactions might cause shame. They aren't conscious of their children's internal experience much at all, which is why they react without thinking.

Therefore, as an ACEIP, is it any wonder that you might feel intensely uncomfortable when you need help from others? The idea of showing your anxiety and needs when you're in a tough spot can feel almost unbearable. You risk feeling like an emotional beggar, soliciting time and attention from someone who doesn't want to give it. It's hard for you to imagine that your vulnerability or need for help wouldn't be experienced as a nuisance, because that's what you learned in childhood. ACEIPs cope with these humiliating emotions in different ways.

For example, you may feel less ashamed if you stay lighthearted or ironic about your need, minimizing how much you need help. You may act apologetic for asking for any sort of assistance, however small. Preemptive apologies reveal your regret about putting the other person in the supposedly unpleasant position of lending a hand. When asking for help, ACEIPs often lead with "I'm so sorry to bother you," or "I know I'm being a nuisance." They hate to interrupt people who they assume would much rather be doing something besides responding to them.

EI parents often cynically suspect that their children's seeking of help is a thinly disguised demand for extra attention. They dislike being inconvenienced and see their children as manipulative. As a result, their response—or lack of—can make their children feel selfish for asking. As an ACEIP, you may have felt that you were always asking for more than your parents wanted to give. It's no wonder you apologize as an adult; you've been taught to doubt the legitimacy of your needs.

Another reason why you may feel bad about seeking help is that you're unfamiliar with altruistic people. When you grow up around self-centered people, it seems globally true that others would not be interested in your problems. So it's not surprising you would think you always have to solve your own problems, even when basic safety is involved.

In childhood many ACEIPs hid injuries, or even assaults, from their parents because they were afraid their parents' reaction would make them feel worse—or that they'd even be blamed for their problem. For instance, one boy crafted a weapon from a piece of sharp wood to carry on the bus after he was pushed around and bullied. His parents were horrified when they found it, which confused him, because what was he supposed to do? Certainly not ask them for help. Another child, a girl, landed wrong on playground equipment and hid a groin injury because she knew her mother would be horrified and embarrassed rather than sympathetic and helpful. Neither of these children could imagine that they'd get any meaningful help from their parents, so they were prepared to handle their problems themselves.

It's possible that once their parents had calmed down from the shock they would've helped their children. But because EI parents react emotionally and defensively to almost everything, these children knew that in times of need, asking for help wouldn't elicit a calm, helpful response. When you're already scared and vulnerable, the prospect of a parent's overreaction is yet another reason not to ask for help.

Another reason you might hesitate to ask for help is that you may worry that others will only say yes because they also have a hard time saying no. You don't want to put them in an awkward position. You may feel that your request will overload them because *you* have so frequently felt burdened by the excessive demands or intrusions of EIPs. But most people with healthy enough self-esteem will let you know if they can't help at this time or if your request is something they don't feel comfortable doing. As you get more comfortable saying no when you want to, you'll automatically find it easier to ask others for help, trusting that they're capable of doing the same.

When help is given in a generous way by adequately mature people, ACEIPs feel that they've been given an enormous gift. They overflow with gratitude. It's hard for them to believe that another person is happy to help and doesn't seem bothered at all. Sometimes friends of ACEIPs discourage their effusive thanks because it feels like they're going overboard and making a big deal out of a small favor. But having considered themselves a "bother," "pest," or "nuisance" for so long, ACEIPs are beyond grateful when someone treats them kindly and altruistically.

Let's look now at how to get more comfortable with asking others for help.

Strategy

Probably the easiest first step in becoming more comfortable asking for assistance is to stop apologizing for needing help. It may be hard to stop prefacing requests with "I'm sorry, but…," yet there's an important symbolic point to this exercise. Every time you resist the urge to apologize, you will be reminding yourself that needing help is nothing to be sorry for. *Everyone* needs help at times. There are other polite ways of seeking assistance in which you don't put yourself down for asking the question. Instead, try saying, "I was wondering if I could ask you for some help with something," or "Would you mind if I asked you for a favor?" You don't have to announce yourself as a bother. You can let the other person enjoy being generous.

Next, think about how you feel when a friend comes to you with a problem or needs your help. Do you find them to be a nuisance or a bother? If you had a child who had a problem, would you want them to keep it to themselves? Or do you enjoy helping if you can?

You can coach yourself out of feeling like a nuisance. For instance, let's say you want to ask a friend to go with you to a doctor's appointment. It isn't an emergency; you would just feel better if you had someone with you. Here's how you could mentally coach yourself through the dread of asking: *We are friends who help each other; he can tell me if he doesn't have time or has other plans. I know him, he'll probably still like me whether he says yes or not. I don't have to be embarrassed for wanting someone to go with me. I'll ask him nicely, and he surely will say no if he can't. I'm not being selfish or attention-seeking here. We're two adults who can communicate honestly. If he says no, I can still be proud of myself for asking.*

It's not selfish to ask for help, but if you're still worried about having done so, you can make a special point of acknowledging the other person's effort. You can send a thank-you text, email, or notecard to the person. You can offer to help them one day, or bring them an unexpected little gift, like flowers or a food treat. There's a whole range of actions available to you around giving and receiving help in healthy ways.

Reflection and Discovery

Write about a time when you needed help but were too embarrassed or uncomfortable to ask for it. Be specific about what worried you about asking for assistance.

_____

_____

_____

_____

_____

_____

Many people keep gratitude journals in which they record things they're thankful for. Imagine keeping a different kind of journal for yourself. Call it "The Courage to Ask" journal. Start now by writing out three examples of times when you asked for help even when it was hard to do. How did it go and how did you feel? Going forward, keep recording moments when you were brave and asked for help.

_____

_____

_____

_____

_____

Tip: It only kills you to ask for help because of how you were treated in the past. See if you can figure out what happened to you. Doing so allows you to make distinctions between your past and your present. When you're encouraging yourself to ask for help, remind yourself that the helper you want to ask is probably very different from the people in your past. Give them a chance to offer you a fresh experience.

Part V

Solving Problems

I'm always nervous about angering or disappointing my adult child.

When your adult child seems emotionally immature

Thirty-year-old Connor had come back home to live with my client, Frances, after several attempts to strike out on his own. Connor had no career or education goals and returned to his widowed mother's home feeling depressed and anxious. When Frances made suggestions about getting his life back on track, Connor became so defensive and angry that they'd both nearly end up in tears. Frances thought Connor would feel better if he chose a direction, but Connor thought her comments were controlling and insensitive to his feelings.

Frances felt that she was doing a lot for Connor by allowing him to live at home, giving him use of her car, and trying to be supportive. But Connor responded to Frances with irritation, demanding his right to keep his room messy and evading chores around the house. He couldn't hold a job, blamed his mother for making him more depressed, and insisted on talking about his problems to the point where Frances felt exhausted. Frances was getting increasingly exasperated: it was one crisis after another, yet Connor wouldn't listen to any advice. He seemed blind to his own role in his problems. Frances felt inadequate to help her son but felt called upon constantly to do just that.

In her sessions with me, Frances showed adequate emotional maturity in her capacity for empathy, self-reflection, and respect for others' boundaries. She had suffered from the emotional immaturity of her parents and self-centered siblings, so she tried hard to make others feel seen and respected. Frances was trying to be empathic toward her son, but Connor's demands and need for attention were wearing her down. Secretly, she couldn't understand why Connor couldn't just pull himself together, get a job, go back to college, or do something other than complain about his anxiety and depression. She'd given him a place to live and a listening ear, and she had secured a good therapist for him. What else was she supposed to do? It seemed Connor just wouldn't grow up.

It's hard on ACEIPs when emotional immaturity appears in their own children. Connor's low stress tolerance, emotional reactivity, defensiveness, obliviousness to boundaries, and tendency to externalize blame made him as difficult to deal with as any EI parent. He depended on Frances for his emotional stability and self-esteem, feeling betrayed when she expected adult considerations from him. Connor was so buffeted about by his emotions that Frances couldn't reason with him. If Frances didn't do what he wanted, Connor would become so angry or despondent that she feared for his safety.

You might wonder how a basically emotionally mature person could end up with an EI adult child. There can be many reasons. Maybe the child had some developmental delays or neurological issues. Perhaps a child's special needs prompted indulgences that infantilized them. For instance, Connor had a condition at birth that required multiple surgeries before the age of ten. Frances did all she could to make Connor feel better as he went through his hospitalizations and recoveries. Frances felt so sorry for him that she often excused his thoughtless behavior, and she held low expectations for his responsibilities to his family and other people. This permissiveness was second nature for Frances because she was accustomed to putting others' needs first and felt guilty if she set boundaries for herself.

If you lacked adequate empathy from your parents, you might go overboard in providing empathy for your own children, trying to save them from what you went through. But if self-sacrifice feels normal to you, you might forget to teach your child about reciprocity and expressing appropriate gratitude. As a result, the child might surmise that their desires should come first, others should show love by always saying yes, and gratitude and thanks aren't necessary.

Sometimes over-permissiveness is triggered because the child's temperament might sub-consciously remind the ACEIP parent of their EI parent's neediness and reactivity. Having been trained to pacify their parent, they may respond to their emotionally reactive child in the same way, unaware that they are perpetuating a type of relationship that will deplete them.

Additionally—although it may be painful to consider—ACEIP parents who've not done their own therapeutic work may not be as empathic to their children's emotional needs and sensitivities as they think they are. If the ACEIP parent wasn't listened to, emotionally sup-ported, or encouraged in childhood to explore individuation, they may find it hard, in turn, to foster their own child's maturational process.

Finally, because many ACEIP parents took care of many of their own needs in childhood, they may assume that their children are as resilient and independent as they were. For instance, they may not realize how crucial emotional closeness is and instead emphasize advice, consequences, or other parenting themes that are reputed to make kids independent and responsible. Having grown up early on their own, some ACEIP parents may not know how to gradually foster independence in a positive way. As a result, certain ACEIP parents may alternate between rescuing their child too often and then expecting them to act maturely without adequate guidance or emotional nurturance. It's hard to hit that balance as a parent when you grew up meeting your own psychological needs alone.

Here are some ideas for how to create a relationship with your EI child in which you are an adult friend and mentor.

Strategy

The best way an ACEIP parent can help an EI adult child is to seek out their own psychotherapy or coaching. It's the best way to change harmful relationship dynamics that may be holdovers from the parent's childhood challenges. Many problems of EI adult children mirror unfinished childhood issues of the parent.

Dealing with EI adult children is very similar to dealing with EI parents. You'll need to see your needs as just as important as theirs, to set healthy boundaries for your own well-being, and to not get caught up in false moral obligations or unhealthy self-sacrifice. Let your EI adult child know that you expect them to think through solutions with you, not just demand help, because you respect their potential to become a self-guiding adult.

You could have a frank talk with your adult child about taking a new direction together, in which the goal is their increased self-reliance over time. Ask them if they'd be on board with such a plan. Explain to them what you can give help with and what your limits are. This will open up new levels of emotional intimacy and honest sharing between you. Be receptive to what they have to say, but don't let yourself get exhausted. Balance between supporting them and taking care of yourself. Keep in mind that the overarching goal is to steer the relationship gradually toward being able to enjoy each other in a mutually adult relationship one day. For various reasons, some EI adult children may always need more attention and support than they can reciprocate, but you'll feel better about your interactions when you claim the right to your limits and self-care.

Finally, avoid pushing your EI adult child to grow up fast by doing a "tough love" move in which you suddenly cut off support. Feelings of abandonment don't strengthen anyone, and certain adult children may have a level of psychological impairment that would make a sudden cutoff feel catastrophic. In such cases, some kind of continuing external support may be a necessity for an EI adult child, but you may not have to be the only one providing it. Give yourselves time to find solutions and outside resources as you and your child work toward either goal—that is, either more independence or finding appropriate support that works for both of you.

Reflection and Discovery

If you're reluctant to set boundaries or say no to your EI adult child, clarify in writing what exactly you fear from them. What makes their behavior so effective in getting you to do what they want?

_____

_____

_____

_____

_____

_____

_____

When your adult child is upset with you, how do you typically respond? Do you have a way of working through a problem with each other, or does one person usually "win"? Which behaviors about how you talk to each other would you change? Could you suggest this new approach to your adult child and invite their ideas too?

_____

_____

_____

_____

_____

_____

_____

Tip: With both EI parents and EI adult children, their emotional urgency will tempt you to sideline your needs and give in to their crisis of the moment. But your unthinking self-sacrifice needs to stop if the relationship is to become healthier and more mutual. With EI adult children, the goal is to offer them help that moves them toward their own autonomy and efficacy, not more entitlement. You can explicitly explain to them the limits of your resources—emotional and material—while giving guidance and encouragement as needed. Helping them find resources outside the home may become an important goal. By being up front with them and kindly communicating your limits, you're modeling for them how people show respect for the needs and boundaries of others. The limits you set are good for the both of you.

40

I still feel intimidated and apologetic around EIPs.

Question the basic premises that all EIPs bring to their interactions

Just like toddlers, EIPs are sure that the source of all their problems lies outside themselves. To little children, it appears that unfair things mysteriously happen to them all the time through no fault of their own. They haven't yet developed the capacity to be objective, so they blame their hardships on external causes, especially other people. They don't see how they affect others, and they certainly don't reflect on how they bring trouble and unhappiness into their own lives. The same can be said for EI adults.

These personality features are especially evident in EIPs who have entitled, narcissistic features, but they can also be seen in the relatively more benign passive types. The passive EIP often pairs with a more actively assertive EIP, riding the coattails of their partner's projections and externalizations. Passive EIPs may not dish out angry accusations or cold shoulders themselves, but they make excuses for the EIPs who do.

Entitled EIPs see a world in which people are either for or against them. Their worldview promotes a readiness for indignant rage and perceived slights. Self-involved EIPs are always alert to signs of being wronged or disrespected, an orientation to life I call the "victimization viewpoint." Victimization, unfairness, and injustice are the central themes and meaning for their life. The plot line of their life story is that someone is keeping them from their best life, and someone else should step in to remedy that injustice. Such EIPs never realize how their demands and distortions are compounding their problems. It's no wonder that the children of these people are haunted by feelings of guilt and responsibility for their parents' unhappiness. An entitled EIP makes others feel that they should fill in for whatever the EIP lacks in life.

Something as small as a difference of opinion can make EIPs with narcissistic features feel that you are against them. When stressed, they can get quite paranoid, believing they're being maligned or forced into things. Their anger and suspiciousness can pressure you to scrutinize yourself for the slightest mistake.

In this emotional atmosphere, it's easy to become intimidated and overly concerned about giving offense. You can't do enough for the EIP because they're not seeking satisfaction or contentment. Instead, they want to prove they're the wronged party, even if they started the trouble to begin with!

No wonder you feel insecure and apologetic. You sense that it's the only mindset that will harmonize you with an easily offended EIP. Just the thought of displeasing these judgmental people is enough to make you do whatever is necessary to soothe and placate them. If you fear them and accept blame, you think you can avoid bigger eruptions. You agree to feel bad about yourself in order to justify their dissatisfaction and quick anger.

In their relationships, the stance of rejecting or entitled EIPs is that they have the final word on reality. They don't wonder about causality or motives; they are sure they already know why someone did what they did. If you find yourself crumpling into self-doubt or hesitancy when faced with an EIP's certainty, it's because some part of you knows that showing self-assurance will probably tempt a collision with them.

To illustrate a solution for dealing with such EI people, let's look at how my client Sam changed his relationship with his rejecting father, so that he no longer felt intimidated or apologetic around him.

Sam's father, Carl, left the family when Sam was in third grade. He lived only a few hours away but kept in touch only sporadically. Although Sam longed for his father's attention, Carl showed little interest in their relationship. Over the years, Sam worked through much of his pain and disappointment over his father's lack of interest and mostly kept his distance. However, when Sam's daughter became a standout pro-soccer draft just before her college graduation, Carl wanted to be invited to her graduation and signing event. Sam's daughter didn't care if her grandfather was involved in her life, leaving it to Sam to decide.

Although Carl postured as a caring grandfather who wanted to participate, Sam did not feel welcoming toward his father. However, he was willing to meet and see if they could find common ground prior to his daughter's graduation. Sam asked his father to give him an hour over a cup of coffee to talk about things and clear the air before celebrating together. Carl balked at the notion of meeting one-on-one, reacting to Sam's request as an unreasonable demand. He didn't see why he couldn't just show up for his granddaughter's festivities and leave it at that.

But Sam didn't want to perpetuate the same unfulfilling, superficial contacts he'd had with his father in childhood.

So here's what Sam did: he considered his needs as important as Carl's, communicated what he wanted from his father, and clarified that Carl was the one saying no. He knew that he was making a reasonable request of a fellow adult. Nothing insulting or outrageous had been proposed. Sam felt a little anxious holding his boundary, and could feel a faint urge to apologize, but he no longer cared if his father felt misunderstood, wronged, or inconvenienced. He hadn't done anything disrespectful. He had simply asked for a meeting that could have paved the way for a smooth reunion on his daughter's big day. He was not the aggressor, and his father was not being victimized.

Carl decided he didn't want to attend the festivities under those conditions. He settled for his granddaughter sending him pictures afterward. Sam was pleased with the outcome because he'd had an honest interaction with his father. Even though Carl didn't want real communication or closeness, Sam felt good because he'd been true to what he needed. By not allowing his father to define the level of their relationship, Sam had interacted with his father as a participant, not just a bystander. Sam was ready for whatever happened next with his father. He didn't feel intimidated or apologetic anymore.

Let's look at the steps you can take so you can interact as a full equal with any disgruntled EIP.

Strategy

First, when you know you're going to need to interact with an entitled or rejecting EIP, prepare yourself beforehand. Think out exactly what you want to say. Write down a basic message that sums up what you want to get across. Then practice your communication by saying your statement out loud three times, pretending you are facing them. You don't have to state your message perfectly, just be sure to reiterate the main points. This practice may be hard and awkward, but it will refine your thinking. Consciously stifle the urge to apologize. It doesn't make sense to apologize for explaining what you need.

Then, evaluate your request in context: *Are* you being unreasonable? *Are* you asking for something extraordinary? *Are* you unjustified in making this request? Anticipate incomprehension on the part of the EIP, as well as pushback. Accept that, through force of habit, a part of you may continue to feel worried and apologetic throughout this process.

Most importantly, don't lose sight of the fact that you're an equal participant in the relationship. It is not age appropriate to adopt a fearful or apologetic attitude with others when you haven't done anything wrong. Recall your "Bill of Rights" (appendix D); under "The Right to Set Limits," you *have the right to say no without a good reason.*

Reflection and Discovery

Who in your life has intimidated you and made you feel apologetic? How do you feel about yourself when you interact with this person?

_____

_____

_____

_____

_____

Write about how it would feel to be able to go through the day stating your preferences, being politely honest about what you like and don't like, without deferring to other people's reactions, apologizing, or defending your choices.

_____

_____

_____

_____

_____

_____

_____

Tip: EIPs may have trained you to bite your tongue and be apologetic for not going along with everything they want. But as a grown-up now, you can claim your right to adult considerations, even if entitled EIPs find your independence insulting. As you communicate your preferences to them, allow them to feel their indignation, discomfort, or unhappiness. You certainly haven't tried to hurt them. All you're doing is trying to take care of yourself. Being nice doesn't mean you have to apologize for your existence.

I'm so concerned about their reactions, it's hard to say my truth.

Remain empowered when EIPs don't like what you have to say

You might find it easy to share your thoughts with friends, and you may have no trouble standing up for your opinion at work, but with domineering EIPs you may instinctively freeze up to the point where you can't speak your mind and then feel compelled to do whatever's necessary to keep them happy. This disempowerment is based on well-founded fears of the EIP's judgment and rejection.

The self-protective instinct to avoid EI displeasure is natural, but silently going along with things with which you don't agree can make you extremely stressed or even sick. Your loss of confidence comes from fearing that an upset EIP will make you pay for not thinking of them first. EIPs often act shocked that you would hurt their feelings by having your own preferences. Their expectation is that you should follow their lead and not surprise them with anything unexpected. Speaking up for what you want or what you think is to risk being judged as crazy, bad, or selfish. No wonder you feel speechless under the threat of this backlash.

The irritability and reactivity of EIPs is legendary. EIPs often have traumatic histories, and this may give them a hair-trigger, adrenaline-charged reactivity to even minor threats. Even apparently small stresses can trigger flashbacks to old traumas, emotionally dysregulating them or sending them on the attack (van der Kolk 2014). Their nervous systems are primed to overreact to threats, even if it's as simple as a difference of opinion.

Animal stress research may help to explain the *why* behind some of this overreactive behavior. Robert Sapolsky (2007, 2012), a longtime stress researcher, reported a series of experiments testing the health effects of electric shocks on lab rats. In some experiments, when rats were shocked and had access to another part of the cage holding a rat that hadn't been shocked, they would go bite that rat. The shocked rats that had the opportunity to bite the "innocent" rats had less stress-related illness than other rats who had nobody to bite after being shocked. The same better health outcome was also observed in rats that had the opportunity to gnaw on a piece of wood after being shocked. Rats even fared better health-wise if they were given a lever to press while being shocked, even if the lever didn't stop the shock.

In summary, the shocked rats that were able to bite another rat or had some other means of active outlet suffered less health damage from stress hormones than those rats that had no outlet objects after a shock. These findings suggest that there was temporary, physically mea-surable stress relief when the rats could "pass along" or dissipate their stress through some kind of action.

It doesn't take much extrapolation to see an analogy to EIPs under stress. In many of their interactions, EIPs act like the shocked rats. They may be redirecting the stress and hurt they've suffered—even if it occurred many years ago—by reflexively taking out their distress on anybody who happens to be around when they're upset. Thus they pass their irritation and pain along to whomever has the bad luck of being in their path. If your EIP never received treatment for a difficult childhood or other past traumas, they may be discharging their earlier stress by picking on you. Once you've been "bitten" by an easily stressed EIP, you may be scared to say anything that might add to their tension.

Aggressive or controlling EIPs act as if they are in a chronic state of stress, like those lab rats, and are doing a poor job of managing it. Whether it's old traumas or current stress, they may displace it onto you by making you uncomfortable or by trying to force you to submit to their control. But it's not your responsibility to endure this "pass-along" pain. It's not your job to restabilize EIPs when they are triggered over a trauma from their past or feel the urge to dump their stress onto someone else.

If you, as an internalizer adult child, have been the object of an EIP's irritability or reac-tivity—or watched this happen to someone else—you may have learned that the wiser move is to prevent any confrontation. Many internalizers have learned to make themselves more accommodating and less expressive, so that the EIP is not so "provoked." Unfortunately, this solution can be hard on your self-esteem if you view your reflexive, self-protective acquies-cence as timid or weak.

But any difficulties you have in speaking up for yourself to a dominant EIP are probably adaptive when seen in the context of past unpleasant encounters. As an internalizer, you might assume that *you* missed something or unnecessarily caused their upset. So maybe your silent shock was the best you could do in the face of EI behavior that was appallingly angry or out of proportion to a situation. However, once you understand that an EIP's intense reactiv-ity might have originated in past trauma and not with you, you may lose the feeling that you did anything wrong by speaking up to them.

Knowing that EIPs are prone to passing along their past trauma or stress by "biting," you can enhance your stress resilience. You can redefine the meaning of the experience and see that it's probably not about you. When you know what kind of behavior to expect from them—their high stress, defensiveness, and externalization of blame—and why it happens, you are less likely to be caught off guard. You understand that their defensiveness and stress displacement are likely due to a painful past and poor stress tolerance. Disproportionate EI reactions are not about you and not likely to be solved by you.

When you understand the possible traumatic or childish reasons why EIPs overreact, they just won't have the same power over you. When you finally believe it's mature and reasonable to speak up for your own preferences, they won't be able to entangle you in their predictable indignation or blowups. Instead of feeling disempowered out of fear of their reactions, you can mentally label their unfair behavior and refuse to absorb their overreactions. The purpose of your life surely is not to be a container for an EIP's trauma, stress, or anger.

Let's look at how you can reclaim your ability to speak up for yourself in the face of an EIP's unfair stress-displacement behavior.

Strategy

Before you respond to a stressed or intimidating EIP, be sure to talk to yourself first. Remind yourself that this EI reactivity may be a pass-along of trauma or displaced stress that you didn't cause. Remind yourself that some of their defensive, intimidating behavior is directed at old ghosts and not at you. Say to yourself: *This much anger could not be caused by me alone.* Make a point of remembering that no matter how an EIP responds, you still have the right to your thoughts and feelings. Remember, *you and your preferences have the right to exist.* You have the right to speak; they can then deal with their feelings about it. You are never to blame for something they imagine you made them feel.

Even if you only *think* to yourself what you'd like to say, it counts, because you're no longer frozen. If you can't speak at the time, you can always bring up the interaction with them later. Emails, texts, and letters can be effective later alternatives when it's too hard to face an EIP in the moment. Timing doesn't matter; write to them when *you* feel ready. When you stop feeling silenced by their unpleasant reactions, you change the false storyline that you somehow mistreated them by being yourself.

Reflection and Discovery

How does it feel when you redefine an intimidating EIP as someone who's doing a poor job of managing stress? Think about how peculiar it is for an adult to get that upset just because you opened up about your needs or opinions.

_____

_____

_____

_____

_____

_____

_____

How does it feel to know that worrying about an EIP's response is your healthy attempt to predict shocking behavior and thereby be psychologically ready for it? How does it feel to reinterpret your anxiety about speaking up around them not as cowardice, but as sensible psychological preparation based on being treated badly?

_____

_____

_____

_____

_____

_____

_____

Tip: You worry about EIP's reactions for good reason. Their defensiveness and invalidation can make you sorry you opened your mouth. But each time you think your own thoughts or speak up, you're affirming your right to have a preference, a point of view, or feelings of your own. You also get practice at being true to yourself even in difficult relationships. Whether thinking your thoughts or stating your truth, you are empowering yourself by not holding things in just to make them comfortable. By speaking up, you offer them a chance to really get to know you. Your relationship will feel very different once it's no longer based on the old assumption that their intensity means they're right.

How can I get through to them?

Communication skills and their limits

First, let's think about why it's so important to you to find a way to get through to the EIPs in your life. If you developed the perfect communication skills, what would you like to accomplish with important EIPs? Perhaps you would know how to start your conversation in such a way that they would be interested in what you have to say. Maybe you would express your feelings so eloquently that they would pay attention and really see you for the first time. Whatever your hope, I bet you wish you could make a connection in which some moments of real closeness and understanding were shared.

If you are an internalizer ACEIP, you probably have already put effort into improving your communication and relationship skills. Internalizers know that being skillful in conversing and listening to people is the best way to make relationships more satisfying and communications more effective. Deeper communication strengthens your bonds and makes your interactions feel more meaningful. You might have been hopeful that better communication skills would improve your relationship with an EIP and bring you closer. But you may have been disappointed. EIPs approach interactions in ways that make communication difficult at best, if not downright impossible.

The effectiveness of your communication is only as good as your listener's willingness to engage, and this willingness will be limited with EIPs. When a person *wants* to understand you, it doesn't matter how you say it. It's equally true that if a person *doesn't* want to understand you, it also doesn't matter how you say it. You can't unilaterally succeed in getting your point across to someone who isn't interested. The most skilled communicator in the world fails in the presence of a closed mind—or a mind that just doesn't see things the same way.

When considering communicating with an EIP, remember that emotionally they are like a young child: extremely egocentric, self-referential, and likely to take everything you say literally and personally. They listen through their emotions and black-and-white thinking, reacting with emotional defensiveness and jumping to conclusions.

You may think you're just sharing your feelings in a clear manner, but all the while they're nervously assessing you as a threat. They don't see sharing feelings and opening up as a desirable way to build closeness. Instead, they may prefer shared activities or larger social events. With little to no interest in the inner worlds of other people, they don't get how meaningful it can be to talk about deeper emotional experiences. Why would anyone feel the need to do that? Instead, they experience such "talks" as boring or as potential contests with a winner and loser.

Besides emotional sharing, many EIPs aren't interested in objective discussion either. Recall that for them reality is what it *feels* like to them, not what is rational or provable. They don't feel obligated to try to follow your line of thought. They'd rather save a lot of time and tell you what they believe—and what everyone else should believe too.

EIPs crave certainty and clear answers. They want things settled, not opened up for consideration, and they have zero interest in considering different angles. Remember that trying to engage them in open-ended sharing may be an exercise in frustration for you. They want to skip the emotional, relational stuff and get back to their certainties as quickly as possible. Not only does this shut down real communication, but it can leave you feeling like you're throwing yourself against a closed door.

For this reason, sometimes you simply will be too tired to try to communicate with or engage with an EIP. You're not being weak if you consciously choose not to engage with them in the moment. There could be many reasons why you don't feel like trying to relate to them on a particular day. You may be feeling a little vulnerable, or you may feel too fatigued to try to get a conversation going. Sometimes attempts to be authentic or to communicate honestly are more taxing than they're worth. You also might avoid discussions with them to save yourself from any anger after the encounter. Those are informed, conscious choices. If you decide to forego the communication effort this time, it's not a defeat. Real connection may not have been on the table anyway.

But in spite of all this, you may still have the occasional urge to "get through" to the EIPs in your life.

If there have been times when they dropped their defenses and briefly interacted with you in an unguarded way, of course you hope to make it happen again. Unfortunately, these moments—when defenses lift and the EIP becomes real for a moment—are rare because of EIP's self-protective tendencies to avoid emotionally intimacy. They are more likely to slip in a moment of closeness when your mutual attention is on a shared activity, the interaction is about to end, there is little privacy, or frequent interruptions are likely. Those connecting moments might also occur when the EIP is feeling nostalgic, or perhaps is facing a life challenge that's making them take stock. But you can't force them to relate. You can only appreciate it if it happens.

Let's see how you might prepare yourself before trying to communicate with an EI person.

Strategy

Communication with EIPs is more rewarding when you're clear with yourself about your goals for the interaction. Ask yourself the following questions before you broach anything with them:

1. Is it important to have this conversation now?

2. What is the one most important thing I want to say?

3. Can I still be proud of my effort even if they don't understand?

Prepare yourself to keep the conversation short and goal directed. Remember, the longer you talk, the less they listen.

Reflection and Discovery

Think about a significant EIP in your life, either past or present, with whom you've had difficulty communicating. What is the one thing you have most wanted this particular EIP to understand about you and your life experience?

_____

_____

_____

_____

What is the one thing you'd most like to hear from this EIP? What have you always wished they would say to you? Write down this precious wish and contemplate what a difference it would make for you to hear it.

_____

_____

_____

_____

Tip: Your urge to communicate in a deeper way is a healthy sign of your desire for connection. But you may be the only one who appreciates your efforts because you may be the only one who sees the significance of what you're doing. Nevertheless, give yourself credit whenever you reach out and take the risk of being emotionally genuine with an EIP in your life. When you do it, you are reversing the trend of staying stuck in superficiality. When you communicate authentically, you at least create the possibility of interactions that could be more fulfilling to you. Whether the communication ends up being rewarding or not, you'll have the satisfaction of having tried something deeper rather than participating in stagnant conversations in which no one gets upset, but no one is really genuine either.

I'm trying to be more assertive, but I keep going along with them.

Discovering the protector parts of your personality

There's something daunting about an EIP who dismisses other people and is determined to get all the attention. They won't take a hint, they won't back down, and they certainly aren't going to worry about how the situation feels to you. It takes energy, resolve, and bravery to be assertive with such a person.

Bridget, a client of mine, felt defeated whenever she had to deal with her overbearing EI mother-in-law, Joan. Bridget often kept her thoughts to herself around Joan, or, if she had a difference of opinion with Joan, she usually capitulated to Joan to keep the peace. She felt like she lost her backbone around Joan and faulted herself for her lack of courage. In our sessions I asked Bridget to reflect on the times she felt intimidated by Joan. I asked her to describe in slow-motion detail how Joan typically reacted to her so she could start to understand how Joan was able to make her back down.

Bridget remembered that whenever she shared an opinion, Joan stiffened and looked at her oddly. Joan also pursed her lips into a thin line and drew her eyebrows together. Her unwelcoming facial expression communicated irritation and impatience rather than interest. If Bridget managed to finish stumbling through her statement, Joan might then repeat Bridget's words slowly, as if who in their right mind would propose such a thing. Then Joan might respond to Bridget's difference of opinion with a "We've always done it this way," or if she felt criticized, she might say something sarcastic, like "I guess I'm an awful person." Days or weeks of tension might follow such an exchange, during which Bridget felt responsible for mending the breach.

Through this initial work Bridget was able to identify each step (Joan's facial expression, the incredulous repeating of Bridget's words, the condescension). Joan shut Bridget down through her emotional rejection and impatience. But once identified, Joan's reactions lost some of their power. When you see *how* someone tries to dominate you, it's not as easy to be emotionally overpowered. But there was more work to do for Bridget to be able to be more assertive with Joan.

Next, Bridget had to uncover the part of her own personality that believed it was best not to rock the boat. Although one part of Bridget consciously wanted to be more assertive around Joan, another part of her felt safer being subservient. Having different aspects to our personality is a normal part of the human condition. (This is not the same thing as having multiple personality disorder in which a person's consciousness switches between internal identities.) But sometimes these different parts create intense inner conflict, as Bridget was experiencing. You can think of the parts of yourself that want to keep you safe as "managers" or "protectors" (Schwartz 1995, 2022) because they automatically take over to protect you from perceived danger.

Bridget had a self-protective part of her personality that compelled her to go along with others, preserving peace in her relationships. As an adult, Bridget knew she had the right to stand up for herself, but under pressure from Joan her internal protector part automatically jumped in and agreed to whatever Joan wanted. I asked Bridget to try and get a sense of the origins of this inner protector and what purpose it was serving for her.

She determined that her inner protector had developed when she was a young girl dealing with an impulsive, angry mother who became physically abusive if crossed. As a child, Bridget learned that standing up for herself only made things worse. Children have limited means for protecting themselves. When they find a response that keeps them safe, they keep engaging the response until it becomes automatic. As adults we may keep employing these inner protectors—as Bridget did when facing Joan—until we deliberately work out new ways of responding.

Bridget had uncovered the protector part of herself, but her work wasn't done. Without the buy-in of this inner protector from childhood, she wasn't going to get far being more self-affirming with Joan. So we continued our work from there, finding out what her protector part was afraid of and working with it to experiment with new behaviors a little bit at a time.

Do you feel like there's an inner protector part of you that causes you to retreat when it's time to stand up for yourself? Let's take a look at how you might get to know this part, and then how you can get its buy-in so you can recalibrate your responses when dealing with domineering EI personalities.

Strategy

Pick one of your automatic responses that you consider self-defeating, something that you wish you didn't do. Instead of being critical toward yourself, consider that some part of your personality initiates this behavior because it was so helpful in the past. For instance, Bridget explored her inner protector by asking herself, *Why would a part of me think it's a good idea to go along with Joan and give in all the time?* Pretend you're interviewing that inner protector part of yourself to try and see your behavior from its point of view. Don't script the conversation, rather let the inner protector's answers pop into your mind.

It might help to identify your protector part with its action slogan. (For instance, Bridget's protector was nicknamed "Forever hold your peace.") The slogan should clearly define the solution that your inner protector came up with when you were young. Naming this childhood strategy is a first step in examining and updating it.

Next, spell out the deeper life guidance hidden within this strategy's slogan. The goal behind your inner protector's action might sound extreme only because a scared, dependent child developed this protective reflex long ago. When Bridget explored the deeper childhood strategy behind her slogan, she came up with two assumptions: 1) *The only way to be accepted by others is to go along with anything they want,* and 2) *People will hate you if you disagree with them, even a little.*

Then write down this old guiding belief on a notecard and read it to yourself *out loud* twice a day for a couple of weeks (Ecker and Hulley 1996). By doing so, you're making conscious and explicit what has been hidden in your subconscious mind as a belief about the safest way to live life. By repeatedly confronting your adult mind with this extreme belief from childhood, your mind will soon want to discard the idea because it doesn't fit adult reality.

Finally, you then can revise the old belief, turning it into guidance that makes more sense. For example, Bridget wrote out her more reasonable adult beliefs as the following: 1) *The way to be accepted by people is to treat them well and find constructive ways of working out your differences,* and 2) *Reasonable people can handle disagreement if you present it in a respectful, collaborative way.*

Translating subconscious beliefs into conscious thoughts helps transform them. You gain power over a behavior when you understand its original protective motive. Now you can understand self-defeating behavior in a new light.

Reflection and Discovery

What do you wish you didn't do when EIPs make you nervous? Describe one of your involuntary reactions that you're not happy with or proud of.

_____

_____

_____

_____

_____

_____

_____

If a particular behavior makes you feel weak, challenge yourself to find its original protective purpose in your life. Think of a time when this behavior might've been the wisest response under the circumstances. When was that?

_____

_____

_____

_____

Tip: Most people just want to overcome or get rid of the parts of their personality that seem to cause trouble. Although it might seem like you'd be better off without them, each part holds some of your vital energy and requires transformation, not demolition. Childhood parts are retained inside us, like Russian nesting dolls, for a reason; many remind us of essential life lessons and alert us to danger. Learn to listen to them, and see if you can collaborate with them to better support your needs as an adult.

Even when I try my new strategies, I still end up feeling drained by them.

Why you feel defeated even when you are successful with EIPs

Once you understand EIPs better, you feel more confident dealing with them. Their behavior is no longer so confusing once you see through their emotional coercions. You can then protect yourself emotionally and they're less likely to overwhelm you with their emotional intensity.

So why does it often still feel so hard to be around them? Why is it still a challenge to spend time with them, and why do you still come away from visits feeling depleted, defeated, and perhaps irritated that you didn't do a better job of not letting them get to you?

For instance, my client Jillian invited her mother for a weekend visit. At meals, Jillian's mother kept feeding the dog from her plate even after Jillian had told her they were training the dog not to beg. Ignoring requests was a familiar pattern of her mother's. Finally, Jillian said, "Mom, if you do that again, you will never be invited back to this house." Her mother laughed it off and made a flippant remark, but she never fed the dog from the table again. Although Jillian had effectively achieved what she wanted, she was left feeling drained and unsatisfied because her mother had blown her off and hadn't apologized.

Interactions with EIPs can also feel exhausting and unsatisfactory to ACEIPs because, since childhood, they have had to hone the skill of what therapist Jacob Brown calls "waiting." For instance, ACEIPs learn in childhood that it's best to wait for their EI parents to be in the right mood before seeking attention, help, or affection. In situations where most people might lose patience and take action, the overdeveloped self-inhibitory reflexes of ACEIPs allow them to sit still and let others take the lead. These *waiting skills* drain energy and promote unhealthy passivity, especially in unstructured social situations such as family visits.

But perhaps you no longer want to passively wait and conform to EI behaviors, such as by letting them take the lead, and you no longer expect your EIP to express interest in your life. Good for you! Yet in spite of these self-empowering developments, constantly setting limits with oblivious EIPs itself can be exhausting. Some people choose less frequent contact not because they can't handle the EIP—they can, admirably—but because being effective takes so much awareness and effort.

Maintaining vigilant self-care is one of those healthy behaviors that becomes draining in interactions with EIPs. That's because even if EIPs—especially those with narcissistic tendencies—do honor your limits, they still are likely to show their displeasure in some way, and dealing with this behavior is tiring. Self-protection, setting boundaries, standing up for what you need, and redirecting one-sided conversations is emotional *work*. As a result, you may come away from EI interactions not feeling very successful, even though you've done a great job of maintaining connection with your self and your limits.

You will stop feeling drained after you stop trying to please EIPs. It's enough that you are in contact with them and are trying to maintain some kind of bond with them. You can't expect yourself to enjoy it too. Lower your expectations and be realistic about how much work and waiting are still involved.

Remember to praise yourself for not losing yourself to their influence completely. If you managed even *one time* to resist guilt or subjugation in an encounter with an EIP, you should pat yourself on the back. Remember, the realistic goal is not to have an *enjoyable* relationship with the EIP; it's to have honest interactions with boundaries in place. Practice being politely honest and genuine, speak up when you can, and end the contact before they wear you out. If you expect the interaction to be enjoyable, you'll probably feel defeated.

Don't forget how much you're asking yourself to do in each interaction with an EIP:

1. Extricate yourself from their emotionally immature relationship system

2. Resist their emotional coercion

3. Keep your distance from their emotion takeovers

If you managed to get through an interaction with an EIP, you made a mighty effort and you know it. Count it as a total success if you complete a visit with anyone who is as insensitive as most EIPs are. These efforts can wear you out. Expecting yourself to feel good about it is asking too much of yourself.

Now let's see how reimagining your goals for EI interactions can conserve your energy and keep you from feeling drained and demoralized.

Strategy

During contacts with EIPs, don't wait for them to show interest in you. You'll feel less drained if you plan things to do that don't involve trying to have a conversation. Use puzzles, games, or handiwork (for example, needlework, drawing, coloring, crafts, and so forth) to occupy you or them while "visiting." The idea is to do something other than direct interacting. Meals are a good activity because sharing food and the cleanup afterward can lead to a sense of conviviality that may not be achieved through conversation attempts.

It's true that EIPs are self-involved and have trouble thinking of others. But it's also true that you might contribute to your own misery by falling into old patterns with them. Are you being too attentive to them? Do you hold back conversationally, waiting to see what they want to talk about? Do you passively endure interactions even after they've become deadening or exhausting?

If you feel drained by an EIP when you get together, nudge yourself with this thought: *It's up to me whether I allow this boring situation to continue. What can I do right now to make this more enjoyable for myself?* You are no longer a dependent child who is seen but not heard. Although you're good at waiting, go ahead and abruptly change the subject. Don't reinforce boredom as a habit. Empower yourself to redirect interactions toward topics or activities you find more interesting.

The more you stop placating and instead take breaks and initiate activities that you enjoy, the less defeated you'll feel. Giving yourself breathing room brings your energy back.

Reflection and Discovery

Think about interactions with EIPs that were tiring to you. What are the things they do that drain you the most?

_____

_____

_____

_____

_____

_____

In interactions with EIPs, how does it feel to spend all your time doing only what they want to do? On a scale of 1 (easy) to 10 (difficult), how hard is it for you to redirect these interactions toward things that are more interesting to you? If it's difficult, what makes it so hard? Write down two things you could try that would enable you to steer interactions in ways you want (for example, being prepared with conversation starters, asking about a specific topic, soliciting their memories about times that interest you, suggesting a different activity).

_____

_____

_____

_____

_____

_____

_____

_____

_____

_____

Tip: As soon as the interaction feels stagnant, you'll know it's time to stop being so attentive to them. If they are your houseguests, you could step outside and be mindful of nature for a few minutes, take a break to go to the gym, ask if they'd like to watch TV while you finish up a work project, or ask if they'd like to work on a puzzle while you take a nap. Better still, encourage them in advance to bring something to read or work on because you'll be needing some time to just relax. If you lower expectations and have these distractions lined up before your get-together, you'll actively prevent everything from being about them. The less passive you are, the less defeated you will feel.

I keep dwelling on how certain EIPs have wronged me.

Anger, ambivalence, and putting obsessive thinking to rest

Human bonds are made up of complex and often contradictory experiences. When you have a close-knit relationship with an EIP, you get to know them very intimately and you attach to them like you do with no other (Bowlby 1969). In the crucible of a special relationship, you will interact with all sides of an EIP's personality, especially if they're a family member or partner. By interacting daily, and on so many fronts, you will encounter their worst traits, and they yours.

Being alternately cared for and then treated insensitively by EIPs or EI family members intensifies both insecurity and strong emotional attachment, creating ambivalence toward them. It's natural to keep turning to those unfulfilling relationships in search of more connection, as if trying to satisfy an urge to cling. For instance, if as a child you needed more love from your parents than what they gave you, as an adult you may continue subconsciously seeing them as holding the keys to your emotional fulfillment.

Unfortunately, when you love an EIP, especially one that's a family member, your heart is like a homing pigeon that keeps returning to an empty roost. You want the love and closeness you may have felt at times, but the truth is, you're more likely to experience their limitations over and over again.

Faced with these frustrations, it's natural to dwell on the ways EIPs or EI family members have let you down, and so for anger to build. Focusing on the anger and sense of injustice aroused by certain EIPs may be an attempt to resolve the ambivalent tension between emotional need and frustrated anger. Instead of feeling pulled apart by these competing feelings, you might resolve the tension by suppressing your attachment to them and focusing only on righteous anger. You build a case against them, becoming preoccupied with their shortcomings, and mentally replay incidents in which they treated you unlovingly or ignored your appeals. You might feel especially justified in your anger if EI family members or other EIPs rationalized their behavior toward you or denied that they did anything wrong.

When obsessive anger causes a frustrating mental entanglement with someone, it may be time to do some excavating to unearth the reasons behind it. For instance, obsessive anger toward an EI family member is usually a potent combination of love, anger, betrayal, and helplessness. Very often obsessive thinking is a cry for help that you're stuck in painful, contradictory feelings that don't seem to have a resolution. In such situations, there are so many competing feelings that your heart avoids pain by leaving it to your head to find a solution. The mind then does the only thing it can, which is to oversimplify so it can think. It obsesses as it attempts to find a simple intellectual solution to a complex emotional issue. Meanwhile, anger serves as a smokescreen for all the other feelings of emotional attachment, betrayal, and helplessness. However, the real resolution lies in exploring *all* these feelings so you can gradually expand your capacity to hold and process such intensely ambivalent experiences.

It is especially painful to process feelings of betrayal and helplessness. Their presence usually suggests that the relationship problems were of traumatic proportions, possibly even threatening your basic sense of existential security. For example, EI parents just don't understand deep feelings very well, and they are likely to let their children linger in emotional helplessness without even realizing what they are doing to the child. Under such conditions, the child's feelings of love for the parents are contaminated with ambivalence due to such excruciating disappointments.

Nevertheless, regardless of your anger and other painful feelings, underneath there may be a child side of you that *does* still love your family member or other EIP and does feel attached, no matter how strong your case for continuing to be angry at them. As you process this mix of love and anger, keep in mind that the inner child part of you may be *overvaluing* what you can get from these old relationships at this point in adulthood.

In the case of EI parents, I've worked with many clients with very happy adult lives and solid relationships who still were preoccupied with trying to win their parents' love, even though their unresolved childhood needs had already been met by their current relationships. It was as if they couldn't give up the fight until they'd somehow forced their parents to care about them. Here's how I explained this dynamic to one woman: "It's like you have a big bag of diamonds, and your mother has a bag of pennies. In spite of all your diamonds, you're still trying to get those pennies from her."

As you process the anger and ambivalence you feel toward any EIP, you might discover that you no longer love them. In fact, you may have moved past those feelings a long time ago, but your anger stopped you from noticing. As the adult you are now, you can and should be honest with yourself about your feelings—or the absence of feelings—toward them. No one has to know the extent of your remaining attachment, as long as you are clear and honest with yourself. Even if you want to continue some contact with certain EIPs, you can do so in the spirit of truth about how you truly feel, accepting for yourself whatever level of relationship they're capable of.

Let's look at how you can be emotionally honest with yourself about all your feelings, so you can stop the mental obsessing that obscures deeper realizations about your true feelings.

Strategy

First, accept the ambivalence that fuels your obsessive resentments about any EI loved one. Expect your feelings to be conflicted when there's so much anger alongside so much love. Let yourself move freely between the opposing poles of anger and emotional need toward this person, articulating for yourself how each emotion is true and justified. Accept that your relationship is full of *both* attachment and hurt. That's the reality.

But once you're aware of both poles, the goal is not to remain entangled in anger or unmet needs, but to grieve your mistreatment and gradually to turn your attention toward taking care of yourself and finding other more satisfying relationships and friendships.

Don't let anger become a distraction from your deeper mission of enriching your own personhood. Keep peering through the aura of invincibility that many EIPs cultivate until you see them objectively as just one more person in your life. Consider that your anger might be artificially prolonging their relevance to you. As long as you are locked in mental battles with them, they never lose their mythic starring role, their halo of emotional importance in your life. Seeing them as big adversaries in your life narrative may be the ultimate way of not *yet* giving up on them.

Sometimes transforming an intense relationship into something more neutral feels like a loss, even when it's done in service of your self-liberation. And it *is* a real loss, the loss of an old dream in which emotionally powerful people finally give us what we needed as children. But reality can provide a better story, one in which *you* grant yourself the rights and powers that let your individuality flourish.

Reflection and Discovery

Think about your biggest grievances against an EIP in your life. What did they do that you are the angriest about? What incidents do you find yourself obsessing about? What emotions might this anger keep you from feeling?

_____

_____

_____

_____

_____

_____

_____

Describe the nature of your ambivalence toward this EIP. Between which feelings do you feel pulled? Make opposing lists of the contradictory feelings you have toward them. Are there positive feelings for every negative one, or vice versa? Overall, what is the tone of your attachment to them? Do you _feel_ love when you're around them, or is it something you _try_ to feel because they were once such a significant part of your life?

_____

_____

_____

_____

_____

_____

Tip: Ask the angriest part of yourself what lies beneath its intense focus on the wrongs you've experienced. Assume this bitter part is hiding something deeper, and you are going to find it. Ask this angrily obsessing part of you what it is afraid will happen if it eases up (Schwartz 1995, 2022). What does your obsessive fixation on anger and blame protect you from knowing, either about your own feelings or about the EIP in question? Close your eyes and sink down into that question. If you discovered that you really don't like this person, how would you feel about that? If you discovered that you do love them and still want to reach out, how would you feel about that? Exploring your combination of feelings toward this EIP helps you make room for all the emotional complexity that has fueled your anger and ambivalence all along.

Do I have to forgive them?

Finding options when forgiveness seems impossible

Forgiveness isn't something you can will yourself to do. It's a state of mind that comes to you when it's good and ready. Pressure to forgive puts an unfair burden on a process that can take a lifetime and may never be completed. Forgiveness is not really a goal; it's more a by-product of years of processing.

You might feel better if you forgave an EIP in your life, but is that a solution you can really achieve? Honestly, is that a solution you even want to achieve? Pushing yourself to forgive might move it even further out of reach.

You may not be able to forgive them, and you may never condone how they treated you, but you may still want a relationship with them. Choosing to maintain a relationship with an EIP doesn't have to invalidate or sweep any part of your experience under the rug. It just says that your reasons for keeping the relationship exist alongside your distress over how you've been treated.

That said, if the EIP is sorry for what they've done, takes responsibility for hurting you, and wants to make amends, forgiveness might come more easily. You sense that they truly understand what they did because they don't say they're sorry that you feel bad; they say they're sorry for *what they've done.* We feel more forgiving toward such a person because our experience feels seen and respected.

Forgiveness is always easier to muster when the other person *asks* for it. However, EIPs don't usually ask for forgiveness because they're sure they're right and they instinctively deny or avoid anything that makes them feel bad about themselves. And since they already pull back from much smaller moments of emotional intimacy, they probably wouldn't extend themselves all the way to asking for forgiveness.

Overall, EIPs usually lack the empathy and self-reflection necessary for a genuine apology. They are so adamantly self-involved with their certainties that they expect you to understand the situation from *their* point of view. They're sure that if you just understood their experience, their actions would make perfect sense. With such a self-justifying attitude, relationships might be more likely to end up in estrangement rather than forgiveness.

Family sociologist Karl Pillemer (2020) has researched estrangement, and he thinks many people don't offer apologies or amends because such an admission would be intolerable to their self-esteem. Although his research didn't identify EIPs per se, his findings on family estrangements is pertinent since emotionally immature behavior of some sort is often involved in broken relationships. For instance, Pillemer found that many people in his estrangement study engaged in what he terms "defensive ignorance," meaning they turned a blind eye to what they did wrong, common EI behavior. Although Pillemer found that a few people spontaneously did apologize later, after the estranged relationship was restored, these people would not apologize while standing in the spotlight of accusation. To me, this suggests that hoping someone will offer an apology or ask for forgiveness is a long shot, and it's especially unlikely to occur under pressure.

For EIPs, this especially may be true because they have limited skills in emotional communication and conflict resolution. If you corner an EIP by telling them how they've hurt you, they may say evasive things like, "Well, what do you want me to say?" They're not necessarily being resistant or surly; they may have no idea how to reconcile because no one has ever shown them how to do it. If you decide to teach them, you might have to spell out exactly what you want them to do: that is, acknowledge how they've hurt you, explicitly say they're sorry, and ask for your forgiveness. You might be the first person in their life to explain how such major relationship repair is done.

What if you cannot forgive? Are there ways to go forward in the relationship anyway? You don't have to forgive them for what they've done, but you might be able to go forward with a new understanding of their emotional limitations and what you are likely to get in the relationship. You could also experiment with looking at their behavior from a more impersonal viewpoint.

For instance, you may find it easier to tolerate them by seeing their inadequacies in a broader context. You could try contemplating them as representatives of the age-old human condition. That is, they handle stress badly, the way humans do, and they often react with defensiveness, egocentricity, unfairness, and even cruelty—traits that are rampant in human beings and have been for centuries. They bang away at other people with their blunt and thoughtless coping skills, and like billions of people before them, they are mostly unaware of the pain they cause. With such a perspective you may shift toward seeing their behavior as more instinct-driven and impersonal—it's not about you and never was—and that may offer a bit more resolution than continuing to try to forgive them.

As you live through your own hard times, forgiveness may become less of a stretch. For instance, some people naturally shift toward more tolerance for others after confronting certain hardships in their own lives. But even if that's the case for you, it's still important to stay meticulously authentic with yourself. Some things in your past may remain too painful to ever be metabolized by forgiveness.

In the end, even if you conjure some empathy for their challenges because life is hard and maturity isn't a given, you don't have to nail that final acrobatic feat of forgiveness. You can recognize your EIP for doing whatever good they have done, without excusing them from the pain they've caused. In some moments you might feel hints of compassion for them, looking at them as psychologically incomplete people who couldn't do better than they did. And yet even so, in other moments you may know in your heart of hearts that a part of you will never forgive them. Struggling with this level of emotional complexity can make expectations of forgiveness seem simplistic and even like a form of denial.

Some people—therapists included—think cultivating compassion for your oppressor is a good way of releasing unforgiving anger. However, this magnanimous approach can backfire. Expecting a wronged person to have compassion for their tormenter is the burden that many ACEIPs were saddled with in childhood. These parentified children (Minuchin et al. 1967; Boszormenyi-Nagy 1984) became emotional caretakers in a role reversal with their parents. They were supposed to be understanding and patient because their parents had such an unhappy life, while their parents were free to keep mistreating them. I believe that therapists shouldn't encourage compassion within an agenda of forgiveness because it's a continuation of this role reversal. The client will find compassion on their own if their truth allows it. Compassion, like forgiveness, is not a goal to be set, but a grace that may—or may not—appear as a by-product of processing one's own pain.

Finally, let's consider one more approach on the subject of forgiveness. In some countries, such as South Africa and Canada, the injuries sustained by one disempowered group of people were too enormous and widespread to be addressed in a judicial setting. Instead, commissions for truth and reconciliation (United States Institute of Peace 1995) were set up to offer oppressed people the opportunity to give voice to the suffering they endured. It's a model that shows that reconciliation can go forward even when the nature of the harm is too great for the perpetrators to expect forgiveness.

Now let's look at how you could apply this idea of reconciliation in your own life.

Strategy

If you're not sure you can forgive, but you'd like to move forward in a relationship with an EIP, you could initiate your own truth-and-reconciliation effort. Explain to the EIP how important it is for you to be heard, even after all these years. Ask them if they'd be willing to listen to your truth, and perhaps offer them the opportunity to tell you their perspective afterward, in the spirit of reconciling for the future. Remember, it's truth and *reconciliation*, not truth and *forgiveness*.

But for truth and reconciliation to be effective, both sides have to be willing to listen, and this is often what EIPs refuse to do. Nor can reconciliation be achieved if one side stays dug in, defensive, and refuses responsibility. If this is your situation but you want to stay in contact, you might give up trying to have your truth heard and instead accept whatever level of relationship seems possible. Pillemer's research (2020) found that many estranged people were most successful reestablishing contact when they maintained firm boundaries going forward and stopped trying to discuss the past.

Now let's sort through some of your own feelings about forgiveness with significant people in your life.

Reflection and Discovery

Think of an EIP in your life whom you respect or love but haven't forgiven for the pain they've caused. Make a side-by-side list and write down 1) the things for which you are grateful to this person and 2) the things you don't forgive. Practice tolerating the complexity of the situation as you contemplate the truth of both sides.

Imagine that this person participates in a truth-and-reconciliation process with you. Write down what you would want them to know about the truth of your experience with them. Imagine what they might say to you if they were able to realize and own what they did. What feelings come up as you imagine such an encounter? How would such an interaction change your feelings toward them?

_____

_____

_____

_____

_____

_____

_____

_____

_____

_____

_____

_____

Tip: You alone know how the person impacted you. If telling them your truth doesn't improve things, do you nonetheless want to stay in contact? If you want to continue a relationship with them, can you let your unforgiveness and unfulfilled need for apology coexist with your other feelings toward them? Do you want them in your life even if they never admit to hurting you or that they were in the wrong? It's crucial to ask yourself these questions because you may never fully work it out with them. Ultimately, only you know if the emotional effort on your part is worth it.

It's sad to think I'll never have a close relationship with them.

Coming to grips with the grief of ambiguous loss

If you lacked adequate emotional closeness with a parent, you may have grown up in the painful emotional state of "ambiguous loss" (Boss 1999). Such loss feels vague and elusive because the parent is physically present but not emotionally responsive. It resembles the uncertain mourning around a missing person, when the ones left behind don't know whether to grieve or not. When you experience ambiguous loss, it can feel hard to justify grieving. It's very hard to put your finger on what's missing. You just feel an odd kind of emotional loneliness.

It's remarkable that people can experience ambiguous loss with people who are still alive and with whom they're still in contact. For example, consider a child whose parent has moved out due to divorce. The child still visits the parent frequently, but the irreplaceable everyday closeness of living together has been lost. Loved ones who are there physically but become emotionally absent for other reasons, such as intoxication, addiction, depression, or other mental disorders, also can create confusing feelings of unspecified loneliness. If you're the child of emotionally unavailable EI parents, you might have felt the absence of empathy and emotional intimacy on a daily basis, also leading to feelings of ambiguous loss.

As an adult, there's another insidious element to ambiguous loss. If you experience ambiguous loss related to someone who's still living, your lingering hope for resolution can prevent necessary grieving. An example would be the healing fantasies about an EIP finally meeting your emotional needs. Although this kind of transformation is unlikely to happen, you keep hoping you'll eventually get what you need from them while overlooking the actual depth of what you've already lost.

If your physical and social needs were met as a child, it may seem hard to believe that insufficient emotional intimacy could have caused you significant harm. As an adult, you might not realize the value of the precious experience of feeling close and being known as deeply real to another person. Such connections are as vital for your emotional health as trace minerals and essential vitamins are key to physical health. Whether child or adult, when you lack emotional intimacy, you may not know what's missing, but you will be affected by its absence nonetheless.

To appreciate how impactful ambiguous loss can be, let's look at my client Beverly's story.

Beverly moved George, her husband of forty years, into a memory care center because his dementia had made it impossible for her to manage him safely at home. Beverly felt scared and sad as she grappled with the loss of her daily life with George, especially because he had always been so affectionate and grateful for her help. After he had been at the facility a while, George stopped recognizing Beverly and no longer told her how much he loved and appreciated her. He seemed equally satisfied regardless of who paid attention to him, and there was no longer anything special about the way he related to Beverly.

For Beverly, this was a loss on top of a loss, but she didn't realize it as such at first since the change in him came on so gradually. Losing this aspect of their special bond was one of many ambiguous losses for which she didn't have words. As George stopped responding to Beverly in his loving way, she became very depressed and no longer wanted to visit him. It was too painful to interact with him as a virtual stranger, yet she felt guilty and disloyal for avoiding their visits. She was slow in realizing how deeply George's lack of response had affected her because her depression was covering up her acute feelings of loss. As we talked, Beverly realized the depth of her grief over how much of him was missing now. "How do you get through grief when he's still there?" she asked me.

Although Beverly's situation was due to George's medical condition, it parallels the relationship many ACEIPs have with EI parents they love: the parent is physically there but emotionally absent. Beverly's emotions also paralleled those of many ACEIPs. Though their parent hasn't died, and some days with them are better than others, an overall atmosphere of loneliness and loss can permeate their experience.

Similar feelings can occur in any EI relationship, such as those with a self-centered friend, a distant spouse, or a difficult boss. In any significant relationship, when the reasonable expectation of a satisfying, mutual connection is not met, you will feel disheartened and emotionally alone. Again, you don't have to be able to define what's lacking to feel the grief. Emotional unavailability affects you whether you name it or not.

Like Beverly, many ACEIPs don't realize that they're living in a state of unacknowledged emotional loneliness and unarticulated grief. They don't know what to do with their "irrational" feelings of sadness. There is no ceremony or condolence card for this kind of loss. Without a name for what we're missing, legitimate grief is often covered over by depressed feelings. We can be aware of depression but still have no idea how much grief we secretly hold inside. However, once you can define emotional loneliness and insecurity as manifestations of real loss, you will appreciate the depth of what you've been missing in your relationship with an EIP, and thus begin to grieve your losses.

To lift Beverly's depression, she needed to feel her acute, underlying grief. I encouraged her to face her pain and to enumerate in detail all that she had lost, every little bit of daily life with and affection from George that had fallen away. Even though she wasn't yet a widow, Beverly named and honored the profound losses that George's disease had caused. Just recognizing the reality of ambiguous loss, and enumerating the many tiny losses specific to it, can help one cope with the emotion that is crying out for acknowledgment.

By the way, grieving doesn't have to mean that you fall apart and retreat from daily life. You can grieve internally and quietly as you turn over the events of your life and think about what's been lost. You may never achieve closure around ambiguous loss, but once you accept it as real loss, you open yourself to finding meaning in your sadness (Boss 2021). Your grief is an affirmation of your ability to love and your sadness shows how important relationships are to you.

Now let's look at how you can explore and express ambiguous loss in your own life.

Strategy

Use the two writing prompts below (Ecker and Hulley 2005–2019) to identify some ambiguous losses in your life related to EIPs. The idea is to name them, and to allow yourself to feel them. It can be hard to specify what you didn't get, but remember that what appears to be a small thing may be crucial, especially to a child.

Think of an important relationship in which you didn't get the connection or emotional intimacy you needed from an important EIP in your life. Pretend you're speaking to this EIP as you complete each sentence, telling them what you lost and how it impacted you. Read the prompt, give yourself a moment, then write down the *first thing* that pops into your mind:

Because of how you acted toward me, I didn't get to feel _____.

If only you had _____, *you and I could have* _____.

As you complete each prompt, you may find more thoughts occurring to you. Jot down each additional thought as well. Allow yourself to feel the poignancy of what was lost due to their neglect or harmful behavior. Whether you fill in the one blank or come up with several fill-ins, see if you can start sensing what you lost.

Perhaps you might come up with additional prompts of your own, starting with *Because you...* What do these prompts reveal about what you lost?

Reflection and Discovery

Do you remember a time when someone outside your relationship with an EIP noticed your loss or sadness? What was it like for someone else to show interest in your feelings?

_____

_____

_____

_____

Has anyone ever invalidated your feelings of ambiguous loss by pointing out all the things you *do* have? What did this feel like?

_____

_____

_____

_____

_____

Tip: Once you've named the ambiguous losses you have experienced using the sentence prompts above, take each of the statements you completed and turn them into a goal or actionable step that could help you now get back what you missed then. To do this, you can use the following sentence prompt: *Even though you deprived me of* _____, *I will find more opportunities for this in my life now.* You might have several thoughts to fill in here, so use your journal if you need more space. Once you stop trying to get EIPs to be who they can't be, you'll have more energy to find other people who will be interested in giving you what you need.

48

I've cut off contact with them, but I still think about them a lot.

Why estrangement doesn't resolve everything

Estrangement is not always the straightforward solution it seems to be. At times it may be the best option with an EIP, but estrangement has emotional costs. You may find that even when you no longer speak to the EIP, they continue to occupy your thoughts.

In his pioneering research on family estrangement and reconciliation, social researcher Karl Pillemer (2020) surveyed a nationally representative group of people and found that 27 percent of them reported being estranged from a family member. Extrapolating from this data, if you're estranged from a family member, you are in the company of approximately 67 million people.

Pillemer's research showed that there is often a high emotional cost with estrangement, such as ongoing stress, feelings of loss, pain over feeling rejected, and the continuing uncertainty of ambiguous loss (Boss 1999; see also chapter 47). Pillemer notes that though it's deceptively easy to cut someone out of your life, maintaining that estrangement can take a lot of emotional energy. Furthermore, he suggests that by refusing contact with someone you also run the risk of initiating (or repeating) a family pattern of estrangement, by showing your children that it's okay to handle disagreements with this option.

Murray Bowen, who developed family systems therapy (Bowen 1978), wrote about the phenomenon of the "emotional cutoff," when a person renounces their family before doing the psychological work necessary to differentiate themselves as individuals separate from the family system. Bowen thought that no matter how far away these people went, they could remain subconsciously emotionally entangled, still carrying the internalized influence of the family and likely unwittingly acting out old family patterns in their own lives. Estrangement may be necessary for self-protection of your mental or physical health, but it's not a shortcut to becoming your own person.

Consider what might happen on the inside of you if you cut yourself off from a significant person in your life. Would the other person disappear from your thoughts and memory, or would you still carry them around inside you, struggling with them in a one-sided way? Would estrangement release you from thinking about the relationship? Sometimes you might foster more self-growth by holding your ground with them rather than cutting off contact.

However, sometimes breaking off contact feels like the only way you can live by your own values and develop yourself as an individual free of their emotional coercion. If you know this is what you're trying to accomplish through estrangement, then giving yourself the room to become your own person can be productive. However, if you break off impulsively, in anger or rejection, you may escape the conflict but not do the personal work that could support your new and stronger sense of identity. Plus, if you haven't yet processed your family dynamics, you may be drawn to new people who turn out to be just as controlling or difficult as the ones you left behind. Separation superficially resembles independence, but only self-knowledge builds a mature individuality.

Estrangement often feels necessary when an EIP's behavior is abusive, intrusive, controlling, demanding, or otherwise toxic. There might be an explosive argument that ends the relationship, or perhaps the EIP keeps ignoring boundaries and won't control their behavior. Maybe they're so self-centered that you no longer want to fight the losing battle to be recognized as an individual. Or perhaps you're just exhausted from constantly holding your own against their insistence on having their way.

If you are estranged and keep thinking about the relationship, perhaps it's time to evaluate if the estrangement has improved your life as you had hoped. A continuing preoccupation with the EIP may mean that you remain emotionally entangled and are still struggling to free yourself from their internalized influence. If you realize you're mentally distracted in this way, it's a great time to seek out therapy, for your sake and for future generations.

If you're considering reestablishing contact with an already estranged EI family member, it's a good idea to reflect on a few questions. Would you be willing to reengage with them if you could keep an optimal distance? How about if you set firm limits on specific behaviors, or started responding to their behavior in more self-protective ways? Estranged or not, you always have the last word on the parameters of any relationship you're in, as well as frequency of contact.

Instead of worrying about whether they'll change their behavior, think about how *your* mindset would need to change to make it safe for you to reestablish contact. One day, when you know you can hold on to your autonomy and self-esteem in spite of them, you may feel ready to engage them again. Or you may prefer not to.

Ask yourself if you *ever* see yourself reconnecting. If the answer is yes, are there any advantages to waiting longer? Are there any advantages to making contact now? Timing may be important to your decision. (Pillemer's book *Fault Lines* has excellent ideas about ways to initiate reconciliation if and when you're ever ready.)

However, if you feel *pressured* by an EIP to engage in what feels like a premature reconciliation, step back and reexamine your readiness to reconnect. Perhaps you do want to make contact, but only if it feels freely chosen. The goal should be to reengage, not reentangle.

Nevertheless, some EI people are so difficult, creepy, or aggressive that renewing contact is never going to be an option. If you feel uncomfortable around them, you have the absolute right to stay away. You have the right to distance from them if they ignore your boundaries or keep trying to control you. You have the right to stay away from them if they did things you'll never recover from. You have the right to stay away from them—period. It doesn't have to be the "right" reason, just your reason.

Now let's turn our attention to considering if a current estrangement is serving you, and whether you want to maintain it.

Strategy

Sorting through your thoughts and feelings in writing will reveal if anything feels emotionally unfinished to you. For example, what exact behaviors would they have to change for you to accept contact again? How would your responses have to change to protect yourself emotionally around them?

If you have repetitive thoughts or internal conversations with estranged people, this is happening for a reason. Try to approach your nagging thoughts with curiosity and compassion, not annoyance. For instance, you might find out that a part of you is missing the attachment, even though they drive you crazy. Acknowledge this as the emotional wish of *one* part of you. Then, ask that emotionally attached part of you to step back while you ask bigger, more objective questions of your true self (Schwartz 1995, 2022): Was it the right move to break it off? Do you regret it? Do you want to change your mind? Do you feel prepared to deal with them now? Do you feel better with no contact? Answering these questions helps clarify why you're having frequent thoughts about them.

Reflection and Discovery

If you are estranged from an EIP, is there an emotional price you've paid for the estrangement?

_____

_____

Did you tell the person what was wrong before you discontinued contact? Why or why not? (No judgment here; you undoubtedly had very good reasons either way.)

_____

_____

_____

Is there anyone in your life with whom you'd like to reestablish contact? What specific terms for the relationship would have to be in place before you'd be willing to reengage with them?

_____

_____

_____

_____

Tip: No one can claim a right to your company; it's your choice. Trust your instincts about whether or not to maintain an estrangement. Even if you don't understand everything about the relationship, discomfort in their presence is enough reason to keep your distance. If the estrangement feels necessary for your continuing growth and stability, there's your answer. But sometimes estrangement feels like a forced choice because you feel unable to assert yourself within a relationship. If that's the case, you may want to work on gaining confidence and authentically expressing yourself to them before giving up a good opportunity to practice these skills.

49 I'm noticing EI behaviors in myself.

How to deal with your inner EI tendencies

I hope you'll keep in mind that we all act emotionally immature at times, especially when we're sick, fatigued, or highly stressed. The question is whether you show signs of emotional immaturity mostly under duress, or if these are the ways in which you ordinarily interact with people. If you're concerned about being emotionally immature yourself, let's review some hallmark EI characteristics and see if they apply to you.

Egocentrism: Human beings tend to be preoccupied with their own interests, but EI egocentrism is different. "Egocentrism" means you focus on yourself to the point of overlooking other people. You don't recognize that although other people are different from you, they're equally significant. You reflexively make yourself the focus of any interaction. In groups, you tell your personal stories to the exclusion of being curious about others. In individual conversations, you usually end up interjecting your favorite topics even if the other person came to you with a problem.

Lack of empathy: When you lack empathy, you don't imagine other people's feelings or consider what their life is like. You don't have much patience for other people's problems and don't think much about how others react to you. You are surprised when people get upset with you for not considering their feelings. You've made statements like "I'm just telling you what I think," "Can't I express an opinion?" and "Why are you so sensitive?"

Very limited self-reflection: EIPs rarely look at themselves objectively. You don't question your actions and usually don't wonder if you've contributed to a problem. Instead, you tend to blame others or external circumstances. You always defend your actions, even if the other person is asking for your apology.

Emotion-mediated reality (Barrett and Bar 2009): If you are an EIP, reality is what you *feel* at the moment, based on the opinions you hold. Instead of checking facts and seeking objective feedback, you insist that reality is the same as *your* viewpoint. You enjoy promoting your beliefs and rarely question them. If people don't agree with your view of reality, your inclination is to get irritated, declare your beliefs more forcefully, and point out that they don't know what they're talking about.

Avoidance of emotional intimacy: If you're emotionally immature, you feel uncomfortable when others want to talk about emotions or their relationship with you. When people try to share their deeper feelings with you, you're likely to change the subject as soon as possible. For instance, if your child is upset or scared, you might reassure them that there's nothing to be upset about, encourage them to move past it, or tell them not to worry. If someone tells you they're unhappy with you, you're likely to start an argument or go off on a tangent. You think emotional sharing is overrated and hate it when people keep bringing this stuff up.

Do you see yourself in any of these characteristics? If so, the fact that you are self-reflective enough to think about your behavior is a good sign that you may be ready for more emotional maturity.

All of us are still maturing, and most of us have engaged in cringeworthy behaviors in the past. For instance, you might try to be a sensitive, empathic parent most of the time but find yourself snapping at your child or overreacting to their mistakes when you're tired or stressed. Or you might be a considerate partner most of the time but micromanage your mate when your task goal of perfection is threatened. Many such regrettable behaviors relate to something done to us earlier in life that we wouldn't deliberately choose to do to our loved ones. Yet there's no denying when we pass this hurt along and harm our relationships in the process.

That said, worrying about being emotionally immature suggests that you aren't deeply emotionally immature. Most EIPs don't self-reflect or worry about how they've treated others. EIPs defend their lapses, but more mature people try to make up for actions that hurt someone.

To increase your emotional maturity, you can resolve to change inconsiderate behaviors and start making amends. You can stop EI behavior with self-examination, with insight, and by hitting the pause button before launching into defensive, self-justifying reactions. With practice, you can catch yourself when you're tempted to engage in impulsive behaviors you learned from the EIPs in your life. With time, old reactions will fade out as you decide to be different. By deliberately choosing more responses, you lay down new neural pathways in your brain that will become as automatic as your original impulses.

Now let's look at how to take steps toward more mature living.

Strategy

Check yourself to see if there are EI behaviors you want to stop engaging in with other people. If there are, make a solemn resolution to never again treat them that way, even if you don't know what the alternative is. For instance, one client set a rule for herself that she would not hit her child, and another decided that he would never again walk out on his wife when they had a difference of opinion. Both of these people had awkward moments as they changed their patterns, because initially they had no idea what to do instead. However, stopping cold your EI behavior guarantees that you will figure out a different response sooner or later. In the interim, you can tell the other person that you're unsure how to respond in the moment and need time to think about it.

In addition, as mentioned earlier, it helps to think of your personality as consisting of different parts that possess *varying levels of maturity* (Schwartz 1995, 2022). (Remember those Russian nesting dolls?) Some aspects of your personality may show astonishing immaturity, needing your help in upgrading their responses. Just like EIPs, these young parts have no idea there's anything wrong with how they react. Your observing adult self can point out the problem and work with them to find a better way.

If you find emotionally immature behaviors in your repertoire, try tracing where they came from and clarifying why you want to change them. Many times, we blindly repeat family behaviors that we unwittingly copied into our handbook of how to be human. Some of your reactions may have come straight from an EI parent in childhood, and until recently you may not have been aware that you were imitating them. You copied their undesirable behavior because it seemed normal. Even when you know better as an adult, you may revert to this old behavior when confronted with surprise or fear.

The more you are willing to reconsider your old behavior and apologize for it, the more mature you will become. You may need both compassion and toughness when dealing with the emotionally immature parts of yourself: compassion for how a part of you learned EI behavior by being subjected to it, and toughness to stop letting reactivity get the better of you again. Don't be too hard on yourself if you can't change as quickly as you'd like. Slow and steady makes it stick.

Reflection and Discovery

Think about a time when you reacted in an emotionally immature way. Describe the reactive emotion that flared up before you responded. What did you do and how do you wish you had responded differently?

_____

_____

_____

_____

_____

Describe an EI thought pattern or behavior to which you're still prone and are willing to give up going forward. Will you commit to catching this behavior and preparing a response to replace it?

_____

_____

Tip: If your behavior has alienated someone, you can fix this. Prepare yourself emotionally to be nondefensive, and then ask if they'd be willing to tell you how you may have hurt them in the past. Listen to the whole thing without defending yourself _even one time_. This will be extremely hard to do, but it's easier if you take notes, bring a supportive friend to coach you, or limit the conversation to a manageable length of time.

Resisting the urge to defend, explain, or strike back may be hard, but you might be able to improve the relationship if you treat this person with respect, interest, and a desire to make peace. You can ask them later if they'd be willing to hear your _five-minute_ side of the story, but only after you have fully respected their point of view. Your brief side of the story is not meant to convince them of anything, but only to complete the communication between the two of you. Your empathy and respect will not just repair the past, it will create a whole new template for your relationship going forward.

They don't take center stage in my mind anymore.

When the spell is broken and you're more interested in other things

Once you deeply understand EIPs, it will be easier to emotionally disentangle from them. You will protect your well-being as something precious now that your selfhood feels just as important to you as theirs. You will no longer react with guilt, shame, or intimidation in response to their emotional coercions. When this time comes, your emotional entanglement ends quietly with a distinct internal shift.

Many people I've worked with can pinpoint the moment they stopped reacting to an EIP in the same old way. Some recall a feeling of interior change, as if something had snapped inside, or as if an immutable barrier had slid into place. Others noticed that for the first time they were left strangely cold by the person's complaints, or simply realized they hadn't thought about a particular EIP for quite a while.

These are the emotional and physical sensations of irreversible emotional differentiation from an EIP. Your self-possession no longer feels probationary; it's yours to keep. And the best thing is, it seems possible to maintain because you no longer feel obliged to see things their way.

How can things shift so profoundly inside you, and why does it feel so final? The sensation of something snapping inside happens when your accumulating consciousness of self reaches critical mass. The sharpness of your realization pops the EIP's overinflated emotional delusions, judgments, and domination. The pact is dissolved, the spell is broken, the debt is rescinded. All that worry, guilt, or distress now feel tiresome.

When you emotionally individuate from EIPs, you end self-sacrifice and no longer feel bad about calculating their demands' costs to you. Accusations of selfishness or disloyalty don't sting anymore because you no longer buy into them. Now that you think like an individual person, not someone ruled by emotional entanglements, it would seem odd if you *didn't* think of yourself and your needs in the relationship.

Like every toddler, EIPs try to convince you—on pain of tantrum—that the world *should* revolve around what they think is right. But once your internal shift happens, their tantrum—for example, their guilt trip, anger, hurt feelings, entitlement, and so forth—feels more like something to be moved through and left behind, not something to be accommodated. Just as a toddler doesn't control your moods or self-esteem after their meltdown has passed, neither does an EIP. Their tantrum becomes an unpleasant part of the day's landscape that you feel no desire to worry about. You don't particularly care about their reactions, and your main desire is to disengage and get back to your life. They no longer hold center stage in your heart and mind as you struggle to make sense out of nonsense.

After you shift inside, their old maneuvers lose their power. Their grievances make them sound like a peevish person complaining and blaming instead of like an abandoned, mistreated puppy needing rescue. Now you easily question their perspective, which is no longer the touchstone of your reality. Best of all, you lose the sense of urgency that their discomfort used to stir up in you. Your ability to detach and observe halts your pattern of self-sacrifice, as well as any compulsion to make them feel important or in control.

Now let's review how you get to the point of pulling away emotionally and what comes after.

Relationships with actively complaining EIPs are unusually draining and often turn into an unpleasant struggle if you try to help them feel better. They seem to seek soothing, but they reject support and advice while implying you don't do enough to help. Interacting with someone who's primed to feel wronged and disrespected is frustrating. Your differentiating moment may come when you realize that complaining is something they enjoy and is not really an appeal for you to rescue them.

More cooperative and passive EIPs may be less demanding and seem easygoing or even stoic. But they can be very emotionally frustrating as well if you try for a more meaningful relationship with them, chasing something deeper than nice times or pleasantries. With each attempt at closeness, passive EIPs get slipperier, like they don't understand what you're getting at. With passive EIPs, your differentiating moment may come when you finally accept that what you see is all you'll ever get. The reason the deeper connection doesn't happen is because they live in shallow waters. When you fully realize this, working so hard to create a connection loses its appeal.

Once you've disentangled yourself from an EIP, you can fill in the spaces in your life that you used to reserve for them in case they needed you. In the process of reclaiming your right to be yourself, your own feelings begin to feel important. You can feel your inner guidance start to kick in. By noticing what hurts and questioning self-suppressive social norms (such as not talking back to parents, always listening politely, putting other people first) that unjustifiably elevate the needs of EIPs above everyone else's, you will stop mindlessly taking on their problems as your own.

You know you're getting free from emotional entanglement with EIPs when your own life starts feeling more interesting than your resentment of them. As you disentangle, you increasingly want to create a life of your own, with your own freely chosen responsibilities and enjoyments. You see them more dispassionately and you no longer feel obliged to hold them at the center of your thoughts and loyalties. Edward St Aubyn beautifully expresses this emerging emotional freedom in the following passage from his novel, *Some Hope*:

> Only when he could hold in balance his hatred and his stunted love, looking on his father with neither pity nor terror but as another human being who had not handled his personality especially well; only when he could live with the ambivalence of never forgiving his father for his crimes but allowing himself to be touched by the unhappiness that had produced them as well as the unhappiness they had produced, could he be released, perhaps, into a new life that would enable him to live instead of merely surviving. He might even enjoy himself. (1994, 177)

Now let's take a look at how you might put yourself first, step away from a draining enmeshment with an EIP, and give yourself permission to pursue more rewarding things in life.

Strategy

Once you know that EIPs' behavior comes from immaturity, it's hard to have the same awed emotional reactions to it. You can make it a point to be unimpressed by their emotional reactivity. See their generalized irritability as a habitual stance, based on their insistence to be right about everything, and not as a judgment of you as a person. Notice how their drama now doesn't seem genuine and no longer pulls you in. Stay in your own shoes as a separate, real person observing the show. Your hard work at self-awareness and learning about EIPs means that old patterns and traumas will no longer trigger or entangle you.

As the EIP loses their central place in your life, be on the lookout for more interesting things and people to do them with. You might feel at a loss sometimes, waiting for your mind to catch up to the new reality of your freedom. However, this won't last for long, as you discover what your true self really enjoys. Look for the people and activities that raise your energy, and don't expect more of yourself than you can freely give. Let yourself be inspired to try something new, or just to do more of the things you already enjoy with less guilt. Remember to claim your right to thrive, not just survive.

Reflection and Discovery

When you get a phone call or message from an EIP in your life, what do you feel? Do you go on alert? Worry about what's coming next? Dread having to act interested while you listen to them?

_____

_____

Imagine how you would *like* to feel when you hear from this person. What would it be like if they didn't stir up any anxiety in you? What would it be like to just be yourself with them?

_____

_____

_____

Now imagine and describe how you would *see yourself* in that relationship in order to be free of that anxiety.

_____

_____

_____

_____

_____

_____

_____

_____

Tip: You can still care about an EIP, but in a less enmeshed way. Detaching doesn't mean losing all feeling for them, but rather the feeling of obligatory fusion that has made it hard for you to be your own person around them. Once you no longer feel so triggered or controlled by them, you can be honest with yourself about how you feel. You might discover that you still care about them but have stopped believing they have the right to come first all the time. Or perhaps you'll find you don't like them at all and have never felt real love for them. It all just becomes part of a truth that you can now accept. As you mature your own self, your feelings are no longer dictated by other people's emotional systems. If you want to continue the relationship with them, you can, but they are no longer the obligatory center of your life. Many more interesting things await you, now that you have stopped worrying so much about displeasing them or figuring out how to get them to be more considerate of you. Why not redirect your energy toward finding those adequately emotionally mature people who can make your life more vibrant and interesting with their wisdom, help, interest, and vitality?

Epilogue

To sum up, let's look at how positive the adult relationship can be between adequately emotionally mature parents and their adult children. Here's a story about a mature father, Lev, his adult daughter, Lana, and a big problem she had.

Lana had just broken up with her live-in boyfriend. He left and took all the furniture from their apartment with him. Since Lana had bought the furniture, she was outraged. She called her dad, Lev, and begged him to help her get her furniture back. Lev listened carefully to her feelings. Then he said he was on his way and would do whatever she wanted when he got there—but would she think about some things during the time it would take him to drive there?

Lana agreed, and Lev asked, "Did you pay for the furniture?"

"Yes," said Lana.

"Did you pick out the furniture?"

"Yes."

"Do you have the skill set to do it over again?"

"Yes," she said.

"Then you have everything inside you that you need to do this again. The only question for you to answer now is, Do you want to be right or do you want to be happy?"

By the time her dad arrived, Lana had made her choice. Instead of entangling herself further with the ex-boyfriend, she decided to let everything go and start again fresh. Her boyfriend had taken none of her intelligence, ability to make money, or taste in decor.

When Lana and Lev discussed the incident later, Lev explained that the first 10 percent of dealing with any bad situation should be devoted to feeling our feelings and seeking emotional support from someone sympathetic. Then the remaining 90 percent of problem-solving should consist of assessing our resources and figuring out how to proceed. Lana and her emotionally mature dad had managed to accomplish all this together.

Lana's ultimate decision about the furniture might seem to be the point of the story. But turning to her father was the crucial first step, the all-important initial 10 percent of the ultimate resolution. The problem solving—the remaining 90 percent—is effective only *after* you've told a sympathetic person what's wrong. Before you take any action, you need that connection and caring. Reaching out to an empathic person who is totally on your side stabilizes your emotions and strengthens you. Once you've felt heard and seen, you can think more clearly about what to do next.

I hope this book has given you 100 percent of what you need: empathy for what you've been through, as well as the discovery of new solutions and directions for your growth. Perhaps the book itself can be a reminder that there are answers for you, and they're just a page turn away.

Going forward, when you get in a tough spot with an EIP, can I count on you to positively answer the following questions?

Are you just as important as they are?

Do you have the right to take care of yourself?

Do you have the right to be happy?

Do you have the skills to get what you need, even if not from them?

Let them have the old stuff. You don't have to claw back what you've lost. You already have everything you need—and more—inside you right now.

Acknowledgments

Of all the things I am grateful for in this life, my husband, Skip, is at the top of the list. His empathy and support have made it possible for me to pursue my many interests, secure in his love, humor, and kindness. His unflinching rationality, coupled with a deep humane sensitivity, makes him a cherished life consultant not only to me, but to his many friends. Skip, I can never thank you enough for all you have given me, just by being yourself.

To my son, Carter, I want to acknowledge what a superb role model you have been to me in living life to the fullest. Carter, you are the ambassador of enthusiasm for the next fun thing and one of the most capable, well-informed people I have ever known. Thank you for all your love and support. And I am grateful to his husband, Nick, for bringing such happiness into our lives this year by joining our family and sharing with us his deep presence, amazing humor, and warmhearted thoughtfulness. (And thanks, Nick, for the great quote.)

Thank you to my close friend Esther Freeman, who is equal parts fun, support, and brilliance, and my cherished sister, Mary Carter Babcock, who has been my one-person creative support team since childhood. A very special thanks as well to Kim Forbes, whose creativity and keen insight have helped me so much in formulating ideas and clarifying what I'm trying to say. Thanks to Lynn Zoll, chief cheerleader and encourager, and to Barbara and Danny Forbes, whose friendship and unfailing support have made my career as a writer something to celebrate. And as always, I appreciate the positivity and connection with longtime friends Judy Snider and Arlene Ingram.

Special thanks to Jessica del Pozo for her comparison chart, appendix B. I am also deeply grateful to all the podcasts hosts who have given me a chance to talk about my books, and to Bea, for telling me her story at the party in Zermatt.

My deepest appreciation to Tesilya Hanauer, acquisitions and developmental editor at New Harbinger Publications, who set destiny in motion by championing and shaping my book ideas with me so they could find their best audience. She and Madison Davis, developmental editor, have read and reread this work, always seeking a little more clarity and usefulness for the reader. For their monumental efforts, I thank you both. Thanks as well to Amy Shoup for her creative covers, and to James Lainsbury for meticulous copyediting toward a highly polished work. Thanks to James's clarity of thought, hard work, and intellectual stamina, this book speaks even more clearly to the reader. Thank you to Cassie Stossel and the marketing team, and special thanks to Dorothy Smyk and her foreign-rights team for supporting my books literally around the world.

A special thanks to Lev and Lana Sapozhnikov for allowing me to use their story to illustrate what emotionally mature parenting with one's adult child can look like.

I also want to thank all the readers who have spread the word about the books, particularly *Adult Children of Emotionally Immature Parents*. So many have taken the time to call and write to let me know how much the books have helped them. There's nothing more motivating than hearing that your work has touched someone's life. Special thanks to Ryan Bartholomew at PESI and Spencer Smith at Praxis, whose interest in my work has enabled many therapists to get video training in helping adult children of emotionally immature parents.

Finally, thank you to my therapy and coaching clients for sharing with me their struggles through confusing and demoralizing interactions with the EIPs in their lives. Their brave honesty was what made this book, and all the ones before it, possible. Thank you for trusting me to understand and support your growth. It has been the greatest honor.

Appendices

Appendix A

Personality Characteristics of Emotionally Immature Parents and People

Personality Structure

- Very egocentric; self-involved and self-preoccupied

- Rigid and simplistic; not complex inside

- Poor self-development; disconnected, poorly integrated parts of self

- All-or-nothing emotions; everything is black and white, good or bad

- Inconsistent and contradictory beliefs and actions (lack of personality integration)

- Not self-reflective; don't wonder about their part in a problem; little self-doubt

Attitude Toward Reality

- Deny, distort, or dismiss reality if it displeases them; oversimplify things to make themselves seem right

- "Affective realism" (Barrett and Bar 2009); "Reality is what I *feel* it to be"

- Self-referential; everything is about them and how it affects them

- Focus on the physical and material, to the exclusion of the emotional or psychological

- Get lost in the concrete details; miss big picture and deeper meanings

Emotional Characteristics

- Intense but shallow emotions

- Underlying irritability and impatience

- Low stress tolerance, tend toward impulsivity

- More feeling than thinking; do what feels best and relieves tension

- No mixed feelings; little modulation or nuance of emotion

Defenses and Coping Style

- Low stress tolerance, impatient, close-minded, one-track mind

- Strongly defensive and critical of the unfamiliar

- Poor self-observation; can't think objectively about their own thinking or behavior

- Tend toward concrete, literal thinking, or impersonal abstract intellectualizing; focus on parts to exclusion of the whole

- Lack of continuity of self across time = poor accountability; "that was then, this is now"

- Immature coping mechanisms (G. Vaillant 2000)

Interpersonal

- Low empathy; insensitive; often provoke anger and frustration in others

- Don't put themselves in others' shoes; don't imagine their inner world or thoughts

- Can't take a hint; overlook other people's feelings and reactions

- Tend to relate to people as parts, roles, or symbolic objects; don't grasp their psychological realness or wholeness as individuals

- Subjective not objective; reject other points of view; discomfort with differences

- Emotional coercion (induce shame, guilt, fear, self-doubt); emotional takeovers

- Don't do emotional work; no relationship repair

- Enmeshment or superficiality instead of emotional intimacy

- Killjoys: sadism, meanness, contempt, envy, mockery, sarcasm, cynicism

- Poor direct communication, rely on emotional contagion instead; projective identification

- Intense discomfort with deep emotion and emotional intimacy

- Hard to give to (poor receptive capacity)

- Demand mirroring and praise, admiration, specialness, authority

- Role reversals; their children worry and take care of them

- Roles are sacred: role rigidity, role entitlement, role coercion

- Playing favorites; seek people to enmesh and psychologically fuse with

Appendix B

Comparison of Emotional Immaturity and Maturity

Emotional Immaturity	Emotional Maturity
Thoughts about life are simplistic, literal, and rigid. Dislike the uncertainty of an evolving reality.	Appreciate the nuances of life and how things are constantly changing.
A need to control others through guilt, anger, or shame.	Aware they cannot and do not want to control others.
View others as incompetent.	See shortcomings as a part of being human.
Express charm and charisma.	Express warmth and sincerity.
Define self and others by their roles in a binary way: submissive or dominant.	Equitable view of all humans and comfortable without a social ranking system in place.
Poor filters; say whatever comes to mind without regard for others' feelings. Claim it is "being honest."	Share feelings from their own experience in mutually respectful ways.
Poor listeners, unattuned, and unable to resonate with others who disagree with them.	Deep listeners, meaning focused, able to attune to self and others.
Resist and deny reality, especially when it does not fit with their opinions.	Integrate new information with acceptance even if it is uncomfortable.
"Affective realism"—things are as they feel at the moment.	The facts do not change because they experience intense feelings.
Unable to learn from errors because actions are not connected as a possible cause of harm to others.	Can self-correct and grow, owning and learning from mistakes.

Emotional Immaturity	Emotional Maturity
Fundamentally fearful and insecure.	Sense of self strong enough to self-regulate emotional safety.
Defend what is familiar because complexity is overwhelming.	Open to changing their minds when new information comes to light.
Do not trust or desire to learn or comprehend complex concepts.	Enjoy learning even if it contradicts what they already believe.
Rigid about rules but change the rules when it benefits them.	Place people before rules, live in grace, can identify ideology and dogma.
Proud of being unyielding and judgmental and consider their rigid thinking moral fortitude.	Flexibility in thinking patterns. Able to update opinions based on new information.
Use superficial logic to shut down other people's feelings. "You shouldn't feel that way because…"	Accept that others feel what they feel.
Believe that if only others would plan well enough, they can avoid all mistakes, and others should always feel bad about their mistakes.	Believe that mistakes are a normal part of life. Able to own mistakes and make sincere repair attempts for healing and growth.
See other people's boundaries as something to overcome.	See other people's boundaries as healthy and something to respect.
Dismiss or scoff at personal growth. Are threatened by the suggestion they are not perfect.	Enjoy the journey of personal growth. Aware they are imperfect and loveable.

Appendix C

The EIP Unspoken Relationship Contract

To remain in good standing with emotionally immature people, I consent to the following:

1. I agree that your needs should come before anyone else's.

2. I agree not to speak my own mind when I'm around you.

3. Please say anything you want, and I won't object.

4. Yes, I must be ignorant if I think differently from you.

5. Of course you should be upset if anyone says no to you about anything.

6. Please educate me about what I should like or dislike.

7. Yes, it makes sense for you to decide how much time I should want to spend with you.

8. You're right, I should show you "respect" by disowning my thoughts in your presence.

9. Of course you shouldn't have to exercise self-control if you don't feel like it.

10. It's fine if you don't think before you speak.

11. It's true: you should never have to wait or deal with any unpleasantness.

12. I agree, you shouldn't have to adjust when circumstances change around you.

13. It's okay if you ignore me, snap at me, or don't act glad to see me. I'll still want to spend time with you.

14. Of course you are entitled to be rude.

15. I agree that you shouldn't have to take directions from anyone.

16. Please talk as long as you like about your favorite topics; I'm ready to just listen and never be asked any questions about myself.

Reprinted from L. Gibson (2019). *Recovering from Emotionally Immature Parents: Practical Tools to Establish Boundaries and Reclaim Your Emotional Autonomy.* Oakland, CA: New Harbinger Publication (178–179).

Appendix D

Bill of Rights for Adult Children of Emotionally Immature Parents

1. The Right to Set Limits

I have the right to set limits on your hurtful or exploitative behavior.

I have the right to break off any interaction in which I feel pressured or coerced.

I have the right to stop anything long before I feel exhausted.

I have the right to call a halt to any interaction I don't find enjoyable.

I have the right to say no without a good reason.

2. The Right Not to Be Emotionally Coerced

I have the right to not be your rescuer.

I have the right to ask you to get help from someone else.

I have the right to not fix your problems.

I have the right to let you manage your own self-esteem without my input.

I have the right to let you manage your own distress.

I have the right to refuse to feel guilty.

3. The Right to Emotional Autonomy and Mental Freedom

I have the right to any and all of my feelings.

I have the right to think anything I want.

I have the right to not be ridiculed or mocked for my values, ideas, or interests.

I have the right to be bothered by how I'm treated.

I have the right to not like your behavior or attitude.

4. The Right to Choose Relationships

I have the right to know whether I love you or not.

I have the right to refuse what you want to give me.

I have the right not to be disloyal to myself just to make things easier on you.

I have the right to end our relationship, even if we're related.

I have the right not to be depended upon.

I have the right to stay away from anyone who is unpleasant or draining.

5. The Right to Clear Communications

I have the right to say anything as long as I do so in a nonviolent, nonharmful way.

I have the right to ask to be listened to.

I have the right to tell you my feelings are hurt.

I have the right to speak up and tell you what I really prefer.

I have the right to be told what you want from me without assuming I should know.

6. The Right to Choose What's Best for Me

I have the right not to do things if it's not a good time for me.

I have the right to leave whenever I want.

I have the right to say no to activities or get-togethers I don't find enjoyable.

I have the right to make my own decisions, without self-doubt.

7. The Right to Live Life My Own Way

I have the right to take action even if you don't think it's a good idea.

I have the right to spend my energy and time on what I find important.

I have the right to trust my inner experiences and take my aspirations seriously.

I have the right to take all the time I need, and not be rushed.

8. The Right to Equal Importance and Respect

I have the right to be considered just as important as you.

I have the right to live my life without ridicule from anyone.

I have the right to be treated respectfully as an independent adult.

I have the right to refuse to feel shame.

9. The Right to Put My Own Health and Well-Being First

I have the right to thrive, not just survive.

I have the right to take time for myself to do what I enjoy.

I have the right to decide how much energy and attention I give to other people.

I have the right to take time to think things over.

I have the right to take care of myself regardless of what others think.

I have the right to take the time and space necessary to nourish my inner world.

10. The Right to Love and Protect Myself

I have the right to self-compassion when I make mistakes.

I have the right to change my self-concept when it no longer fits.

I have the right to love myself and treat myself nicely.

I have the right to be free of self-criticism, and to enjoy my individuality.

I have the right to be me.

Reprinted from L. Gibson (2019). *Recovering from Emotionally Immature Parents: Practical Tools to Establish Boundaries and Reclaim Your Emotional Autonomy.* Oakland, CA: New Harbinger Publication (197–202).

References

Ainsworth, M. 1982. "Attachment: Retrospect and Prospect." In *The Place of Attachment in Human Behavior*, edited by Colin Parkes and Joan Stevenson-Hinde. New York: Basic Books.

Ainsworth, M., S. Bell, and D. Stayton. 1974. "Infant-Mother Attachment and Social Development: 'Socialization' as a Product of Reciprocal Responsiveness to Signals." In *The Integration of a Child into a Social World*, edited by Martin Richards. New York: Cambridge University Press.

Ames, L. B., and F. L. Ilg. 1982. *Your One-Year-Old*. New York: Dell Publishing.

Anderson, C. 1995. *The Stages of Life*. New York: Atlantic Monthly Press.

Aron, E. 1996. *The Highly Sensitive Person*. New York: Broadway Books.

Bandura, A. 1971. "Introduction." In *Psychological Modeling: Conflicting Theories*, edited by Albert Bandura. New York: Routledge.

Barrett, L. F., and M. Bar. 2009. "See It with Feeling: Affective Predictions During Object Perception." *Philosophical Transactions of the Royal Society B: Biological Sciences* 363: 1325–34.

Beatty, M. 1986. *Co-dependent No More*. Center City, MN: Hazelden.

Boss, P. 1999. *Ambiguous Loss*. Cambridge, MA: Harvard University Press.

———. 2021. *The Myth of Closure*. New York: W. W. Norton.

Boszormenyi-Nagy, I. 1984. *Invisible Loyalties*. New York: Brunner/Mazel.

Bowen, M. 1978. *Family Therapy in Clinical Practice*. New York: Rowman and Littlefield.

Bowlby, J. 1969. *Attachment*. New York: Basic Books.

Byng-Hall, J. 1985. "The Family Script: A Useful Bridge Between Theory and Practice." *Journal of Family Therapy* 7: 301–5.

Campbell, R. 1977. *How to Really Love Your Child*. Colorado Springs, CO: David C. Cook.

———. 1981. *How to Really Love Your Teenager*. Colorado Springs, CO: David C. Cook.

Clance, P. R. 1985. *The Imposter Phenomenon*. Atlanta, GA: Peachtree Publishers.

Corrigan, E. G., and P. Gordon. 1995. *The Mind Object*. Northvale, NJ: Jason Aronson.

Del Pozo, J. 2021. "Epidemic Emotional Immaturity: The Deadly Cost of Not Growing Up." Being Awake Better (blog), *Psychology Today*. March 29. https://www.psychologytoday .com/us/blog/being-awake-better/202103/epidemic-emotional-immaturity.

Ecker, B., and L. Hulley. 1996. *Depth-Oriented Brief Psychotherapy*. San Francisco: Jossey-Bass.

———. 2005–2019. *Coherence Therapy: Practice Manual and Training Guide*. Oakland, CA: Coherence Psychology Institute.

Epstein, M. 2022. *The Zen of Therapy*. New York: Penguin Press.

Erikson, E. 1950. *Childhood and Society*. New York: W. W. Norton.

Faber, A., and E. Mazlish. 2012. *How to Talk So Kids Will Listen and Listen So Kids Will Talk*. New York: Scribner Classics.

Festinger, L. 1957. *A Theory of Cognitive Dissonance*. Stanford, CA: Stanford University Press.

Fonagy, P., and M. Target. 2008. "Attachment, Trauma, and Psychoanalysis: Where Psychoanalysis Meets Neuroscience." In *Mind to Mind: Infant Research, Neuroscience, and Psychoanalysis*, edited by Elliot Jurist, Arietta Slade, and Sharone Bergner. New York: Other Press.

Fosha, D. 2000. *The Transforming Power of Affect*. New York: Basic Books.

———. 2004. "Nothing That Feels Bad Is Ever the Last Step." In special issue on "Emotion in Psychotherapy," edited by L. Greenberg, *Clinical Psychology and Psychotherapy* 11: 30–43.

Fraad, H. 2008. "Toiling in the Field of Emotion." *Journal of Psychohistory* 35: 270–86.

Freud, A. 1936. *The Ego and the Mechanisms of Defence*. New York: Routledge.

Freud, S. 1894. *The Neuro-Psychoses of Defence*. Redditch, UK: Read Books Ltd.

Gendlin, E. T. 1978. *Focusing*. New York: Bantam Dell.

Gibson, L. C. 2015. *Adult Children of Emotionally Immature Parents*. Oakland, CA: New Harbinger Publications.

———. 2019. *Recovering from Emotionally Immature Parents*. Oakland, CA: New Harbinger Publications.

————. 2020. *Who You Were Meant to Be: A Guide to Finding or Recovering Your Life's Purpose*, 2nd ed. Virginia Beach, VA: Blue Bird Press.

————. 2021. *Self-Care for Adult Children of Emotionally Immature Parents*. Oakland, CA: New Harbinger Publications.

Gottman, J., and J. DeClaire. 2001. *The Relationship Cure*. New York: Harmony Books.

Gottman, J., and N. Silver. 1999. *The Seven Principles for Making Marriage Work*. New York: Harmony Books.

Green, R. 1998. *The Explosive Child*. New York: HarperCollins.

Hatfield, E. R., R. L. Rapson, and Y. L. Le. 2009. "Emotional Contagion and Empathy." In *The Social Neuroscience of Empathy*, edited by Jean Decety and William Ickes. Boston: MIT Press.

Helgoe, L. 2019. *Fragile Bully*. New York: Diversion Books.

Johnson, S. 2019. *Attachment Theory in Practice*. New York: Guilford Press.

Jung, C. G. 1997. *Jung on Active Imagination*. Edited by J. Chodorow. Princeton, NJ: Princeton University Press.

Karpman, S. 1968. "Fairy Tales and Script Drama Analysis." *Transactional Analysis Bulletin* 26: 39–43.

Kernberg, O. 1975. *Borderline Conditions and Pathological Narcissism*. Lanham, MD: Rowman and Littlefield Publishing.

Kohut, H. 1971. *The Analysis of the Self*. Chicago: University of Chicago Press.

Kurcinka, M. S. 2015. *Your Spirited Child*. 2nd ed. New York: William Morrow.

Mahler, M., F. Pine, and A. Bergman. 1975. *The Psychological Birth of the Human Infant*. New York: Basic Books.

Maier, S. F., and M. E. P. Seligman. 2016. "Learned Helplessness at Fifty: Insights from Neuroscience." *Psychological Review* 123: 349–67.

Marlow-MaCoy, A. 2020. *The Gaslighting Recovery Workbook*. Emeryville, CA: Rockridge Press.

Maslow, A. 2014. *Toward a Psychology of Being*. Floyd, VA: Sublime Books.

McCullough, L., N. Kuhn, S. Andrews, A. Kaplan, J. Wolf, and C. Hurley. 2003. *Treating Affect Phobia*. New York: Guilford Press.

Minuchin, S., B. Montalvo, B. G. Guerney, B. L. Rosman, and F. Schumer. 1967. *Families of the Slums*. New York: Basic Books.

Mirza, D. 2017. *The Covert Passive-Aggressive Narcissist*. Ashland, OR: Debra Mirza and Safe Place Publishing.

Newberg, A., and M. R. Waldman. 2009. *How God Changes Your Brain*. New York: Ballantine Books.

Ogden, T. 1982. *Projective Identification and Psychoanalytic Technique*. Northvale, NJ: Jason Aronson.

Pillemer, K. 2020. *Fault Lines*. New York: Avery/Penguin Random House.

Porges, S. 2011. *The Polyvagal Theory: Neurophysiological Foundations of Emotions, Attachment, Communication, Self-Regulation*. New York: W. W. Norton.

———. 2017. *The Pocket Guide to the Polyvagal Theory*. New York: W.W. Norton.

Sapolsky, R. M. 2007. "Stress." *Radiolab* interview. https://radiolab.org/episodes/91580-stress.

———. 2012. "How to Relieve Stress." *Greater Good Magazine*, March 22. https://greatergood.berkeley.edu/article/item/how_to_relieve_stress.

Schwartz, R. 1995. *Internal Family Systems*. New York: Guildford Press.

———. 2022. *No Bad Parts*. Louisville, CO: Sounds True Publications.

Seligman, M. E. 1972. "Learned Helplessness." *Annual Review of Medicine* 23: 407–12.

Shaw, D. 2014. *Traumatic Narcissism*. New York: Routledge.

St. Aubyn, E. 1994. *Some Hope*. London: Picador.

Steiner, C. 1974. *Scripts People Live*. New York: Grove Press.

Taylor, K. 2004. *Brainwashing*. Oxford, UK: Oxford University Press.

United States Institute of Peace. 1995. "Truth Commission: South Africa." December 1. https://www.usip.org/publications/1995/12/truth-commission-south-africa.

Vaillant, G. 1977. *Adaptation to Life*. Cambridge, MA: Harvard University Press.

———. 2000. "Adaptive Mental Mechanism: Their Role in a Positive Psychology." *American Psychologist* 55: 89–98.

———. 2009. *Spiritual Evolution*. New York: Harmony Books.

Vaillant, L. M. 1997. *Changing Character*. New York: Basic Books.

van der Kolk, B. 2014. *The Body Keeps the Score.* New York: Viking.

Whitfield, C. L. 1987. *Healing the Child Within.* Deerfield Beach, FL: Health Communications, Inc.

Winnicott, D. W. 1958. "Mind and Its Relation to the Psyche-Soma." In *Collected Papers: Through Paediatrics to Psychoanalysis.* London: Tavistock.

———. 1988. *Human Nature.* New York: Schocken.

———. 1989. *Psycho-Analytic Explorations.* Edited by Clare Winnicott, Ray Shepherd, and Madeleine Davis. New York: Karnac Books.

———. 2002. *Winnicott on the Child.* New York: Perseus Books Group.

Wolynn, M. 2016. *It Didn't Start with You.* New York: Penguin Random House.

Lindsay C. Gibson, PsyD, is a clinical psychologist who has been a psychotherapist for more than thirty-five years, working in both public and private practice. In the past, Gibson has served as adjunct assistant professor for the Virginia Consortium Program in clinical psychology, teaching doctoral students clinical theory and psychotherapy techniques. She specializes in working with adults to attain new levels of personal growth, emotional intimacy with others, and confidence in dealing with emotionally immature family members.

Gibson is author of four books: *Who You Were Meant to Be*, *Adult Children of Emotionally Immature Parents*, *Recovering from Emotionally Immature Parents*, and *Self-Care for Adult Children of Emotionally Immature Parents*. She also wrote a monthly column on well-being for *Tidewater Women* and *Tidewater Family* magazines for over twenty years. Her website is available at http://www.lindsaygibsonpsyd.com/. Gibson lives and works in Virginia Beach, VA.

Index

More Books *by* Lindsay C. Gibson, PsyD

This breakthrough book offers profound insight
and practical guidance to help you heal the invisible
wounds of growing up with an emotionally
immature or unavailable parent.

978-1626251700 / US $18.95

This compassionate guide will help you
nurture a deeper sense of self-worth, set boundaries
with others, and live with confidence.

978-1684039821 / US $17.95

🌱 **newharbinger**publications

1-800-748-6273 / newharbinger.com